New Perspectives on

The Internet Using Netscape Navigator™ Software

BRIEF

Sandra E. Poindexter
Northern Michigan University

A DIVISION OF COURSE TECHNOLOGY
ONE MAIN STREET, CAMBRIDGE, MA 02142

an International Thomson Publishing company I(T)P

Cambridge • Albany • Bonn • Boston • Cincinnati • London • Madrid • Melbourne • Mexico City
New York • Paris • San Francisco • Singapore • Tokyo • Toronto • Washington

New Perspectives on the Internet Using Netscape Navigator Software — Brief is published by CTI.

Managing Editor	Mac Mendelsohn
Series Consulting Editor	Susan Solomon
Senior Product Manager	Barbara Clemens
Product Manager/Developmental Editor	Robin Geller
Production Editor	Nancy Ray
Text and Cover Designer	Ella Hanna
Cover Illustrator	Nancy Nash

© 1996 by CTI.
A Division of Course Technology – I(T)P.

For more information contact:

Course Technology
One Main Street
Cambridge, MA 02142

International Thomson Editores
Campos Eliseos 385, Piso 7
Col. Polanco
11560 Mexico D.F. Mexico

International Thomson Publishing Europe
Berkshire House 168-173
High Holborn
London WCIV 7AA
England

International Thomson Publishing GmbH
Königswinterer Strasse 418
53227 Bonn
Germany

Thomas Nelson Australia
102 Dodds Street
South Melbourne, 3205
Victoria, Australia

International Thomson Publishing Asia
211 Henderson Road
#05-10 Henderson Building
Singapore 0315

Nelson Canada
1120 Birchmount Road
Scarborough, Ontario
Canada M1K 5G4

International Thomson Publishing Japan
Hirakawacho Kyowa Building, 3F
2-2-1 Hirakawacho
Chiyoda-ku, Tokyo 102
Japan

ISBN 0-7600-3820-1

Printed in the United States of America

10 9 8 7 6 5 4 3

How does this book I'm holding fit into the New Perspectives Series?

New Perspectives microcomputer concepts and applications books are available in the following categories:

Brief books are about 100 pages long and are intended to teach only the essentials. They contain 2 to 4 tutorials. The book you are holding is a Brief book.

Introductory books are about 300 pages and consist of 6 or 7 chapters or tutorials. An Introductory book is designed for a short course or for a one-term course, used in combination with other Introductory books.

Comprehensive books are about 600 pages long and consist of all of the chapters or tutorials in the Introductory book, plus 3 or 4 more Intermediate chapters or tutorials covering higher-level topics. Comprehensive applications texts include Brief Windows tutorials, the Introductory and Intermediate tutorials, 3 or 4 Additional Cases, and a Reference Section.

Advanced applications books cover topics similar to those in the Comprehensive books, but in more depth. Advanced books present the most high-level coverage in the series.

Custom Books The New Perspectives Series offers you two ways to customize a New Perspectives text to fit your course exactly: *CourseKits*, 2 or more texts packaged together in a box, and *Custom Editions*, your choice of books bound together. Custom Editions offer you unparalleled flexibility in designing your concepts and applications courses. You can build your own book by ordering a combination of titles bound together to cover only the topics you want. Your students save because they buy only the materials they need. There is no minimum order, and books are spiral bound. Both CourseKits and Custom Editions offer significant price discounts. Contact your CTI sales representative for more information.

New Perspectives Series Concepts and Applications

- ■ Brief Titles or Modules
- ■ Introductory Titles or Modules
- ■ Intermediate Modules
- ■ Advanced Titles or Modules
- □ Other Modules
- □ Individual Concepts Chapters

Brief	Introductory	Comprehensive	Advanced Applications	Custom Editions
Concepts and Applications				
2 to 4 tutorials or chapters	Brief + 4 or 5 more tutorials or chapters	1 Introductory + 3 or 4 Intermediate tutorials or chapters. Applications have Brief Windows, Additional Cases and Reference section.	Quick Review of basics + in-depth, high-level coverage	Choose from any of the above to build your own Custom Editions® or Course Kits®

How do the Windows 95 editions differ from the Windows 3.1 editions?

Aside from the obvious change—covering Windows 95 software instead of 3.1 software—we've made several changes in the Windows 95 editions of the **New Perspectives Series**. We listened to instructors who use the series and made the changes they've asked us to make—to make this series even better.

Larger Page Size If you've used a **New Perspectives** text before, you'll immediately notice the book your holding is larger than our Windows 3.1 series books. We've responded to user requests for a larger page, which allows for larger screen shots and associated callouts.

Sessions We've divided the Tutorials into sessions. Each session is designed to be completed in about 45 minutes to an hour (depending, of course, upon specific student needs and the speed of your lab equipment). With sessions, learning is broken up into more easily-assimilated "chunks." You can more accurately allocate time in your syllabus. Students can more easily manage the available lab time. Each session begins with a "session box," which quickly describes what skills the student will learn in the session. Furthermore, each session is numbered, making it easier for you and your students to navigate and communicate about the tutorial.

Quick Checks Each session concludes with meaningful, conceptual questions—called Quick Checks—that test students' understanding of what they learned in the session. The answers to all of the Quick Check Questions are at the back of the book, preceding the Index.

New Design We have retained a design that helps students easily differentiate between what they are to *do* and what they are to *read*. The steps are easily identified by their color background and numbered steps. Furthermore, this new design presents steps and screen shots in a larger, easier-to-read format.

What features are retained in the Windows 95 editions of the New Perspectives Series?

"Read This Before You Begin" Page This page is consistent with Course Technology's unequaled commitment to helping instructors introduce technology into the classroom. Technical considerations and assumptions about hardware and software are listed in one place to help instructors save time and eliminate unnecessary aggravation.

Tutorial Case Each tutorial begins with a problem presented in a case that is meaningful to students. The problem turns the task of learning how to use an application into a problem-solving process. The problems increase in complexity with each tutorial. These cases touch on multicultural, international, and ethical issues—so important to today's business curriculum.

Step-by-Step Methodology   The Course Technology step-by-step methodology keeps students on track. They click or press keys always within the context of solving the problem posed in the Tutorial Case. The text constantly guides students, letting them know where they are in the course of solving the problem. In addition, the numerous screen shots include labels that direct students' attention to what they should look at on the screen. On almost every page in this book, you can find an example of how steps, screen shots, and labels work together.

TROUBLE?

TROUBLE? Paragraphs   Trouble paragraphs anticipate the mistakes that students are likely to make and help them recover from these mistakes. By putting these paragraph in the book, rather than in the instructor's manual, we facilitate independent learning and free the instructor to focus on substantive conceptual issues rather than on common procedural errors.

Reference Windows   Reference Windows appear throughout the text. This feature is specially designed and written so students can refer to them when doing the Tutorial Assignments and Case Problems, and after completing the course.

Task Reference   The Task Reference is a summary of how to perform commonly-used tasks using the most efficient method, as well as helpful shortcuts.

Tutorial Assignments, Case Problems, and Lab Assignments   Each tutorial concludes with Tutorial Assignments, which provide students additional hands-on practice of the skills they learned in the tutorial. The Tutorial Assignments are followed by four Case Problems that have approximately the same scope as the Tutorial Case. Finally, if a Lab (see below) accompanies the tutorial, Lab Assignments are included.

Exploration Exercises   The Windows environment allows students to learn by exploring and discovering what they can do. Exploration Exercises can be Tutorial Assignments or Case Problems that encourage students to explore the capabilities of the program they are using and to extend their knowledge using the Windows Help facility and other reference materials.

The New Perspectives Series is known for using technology to help instructors teach and administer, and to help students learn. What CourseTools are available with this textbook?

All the teaching and learning materials available with the **New Perspectives Series** are known as CourseTools. The following CourseTools are available with this textbook:

Course Presenter   Course Presenter is a CD-ROM-based presentation tool that provides instructors a wealth of resources for use in the classroom, replacing traditional overhead transparencies with computer-generated screenshows. Presenter gives instructors the flexibility to create custom presentations, complete with matching students notes and lecture notes pages. The presentations are closely coordinated with the content of the New Perspectives book and other Course Tools, and provide another resource to help instructors to teach the way they want to teach.

Course Labs Computer skills and concepts come to life with the New Perspectives Course Labs—highly interactive online tutorials that guide students step by step, present them with Quick Check questions, allow them to explore on their own, and test their comprehension. Lab Assignments are also included in the book at the end of each relevant tutorial. The labs available with this book and the tutorials in which they appear are:

The Internet
World Wide Web   **E-Mail**
Tutorial 1   Tutorial 3

Online Companions When you use a New Perspectives product, you can access Course Technology's faculty and student sites on the World Wide Web. You may browse the password-protected Faculty Online Companion to obtain all of the materials you need to prepare for class. Please see your online Instructor's Manual or call your Course Technology customer service representative for more information. Students may access their Online Companion in the Student Center at http://www.vmedia.com/cti/.

Online Instructor's Manual The Instructor's Manual to Accompany *New Perspectives on the Internet Using Netscape Navigator Software™—Brief* was prepared by the author and is available through the Course Technology Faculty Online Companion. Call your customer service representative for the URL and your password. The online Instructor's Manual contains the following items:

- Instructor's Notes, containing an overview, an outline, technical notes, lecture notes, and an extra case problem for each tutorial.
- Solutions to the Tutorial Assignments and Case Problems.

Acknowledgments

I wish to thank the following reviewers for their responses and suggestions: Tim Sylvester, Glendale Community College; Stephanie Low Chenault, The College of Charleston; and Duane Johnson, Des Moines Area Community College. Many thanks to Patrick Carey for his advice and end-of-chapter contributions.

Special thanks to June Parsons and Dan Oja for their contributions and support. Many thanks to the New Perspectives team at Course Technology, particularly Mac Mendelsohn, Managing Editor, Susan Solomon, Series Consulting Editor, Barbara Clemens, Senior Product Manager; Chris Greacen, Webmaster; Jim Valente, Manuscript Quality Coordinator; student testers Gina Griffiths and Carol McDermott; and especially Robin Geller, Developmental Editor and Product Manager, who kept me on track

Without the assistance of Martin Eskelinen, Helen Heck, Jane Phillips, Mike Bradley, and Steve and Anna Poindexter this book could not have been written. Finally, my thanks to Peter Heck who gave me the drive not just to finish, but to succeed.

Sandra Poindexter

Table of **Contents**

TUTORIAL 3

Corresponding with E-mail and Transferring Files

Providing Technical Support for Global Marketers, Inc.   NS 81

Reference Windows

Uses and Abuses

New Perspectives on

The Internet Using Netscape Navigator™ Software

BRIEF

TUTORIALS

Read This **Before You Begin**

STUDENT DISKS

To complete the tutorials, Tutorial Assignments, and Case Problems in this book, you need three blank, formatted high-density disks, which you will use to store files that you save and download in the tutorials. In order to make sure you have enough room on each disk, label and use the disks according to this table:

Disk	Write this on the disk label
1	Student Disk 1: Sessions 2.1, 2.2, and 3.1
2	Student Disk 2: Session 3.2
3	Student Disk 3: Tutorial 3 Case Problem 3

When a tutorial tells you to use a Student Disk, be sure you use the correct disk. Session 1.1 directs you to open a file, but this should be installed on your network server by your instructor or technical support person. It is not a file on your Student Disk.

COURSE LABS

This book features two interactive Course Labs to help you understand Internet World Wide Web and e-mail concepts. There are Lab Assignments at the end of Tutorials 1 and 3 that relate to these labs. **To start the Labs using Windows 95**, click the Start button on the Windows 95 taskbar, point to Programs, point to Course Labs, point to New Perspectives Applications and click the name of the lab you want to use. **To start the Labs using Windows 3.1**, double-click the Course Labs for the Internet group icon to open a window containing the Lab icons, then double-click the icon for the Lab you want to use.

USING YOUR OWN COMPUTER

If you are going to work through this book using your own computer, you need:

■ **Computer System** A system that enables you to access Netscape Navigator 2.0. You may use either Windows 3.1 or Windows 95 to access Netscape Navigator. The screens in this book show Netscape Navigator running under Windows 95. However, you will still be able to use this book successfully under Windows 3.1. Trouble? paragraphs throughout the book note differences you may see if you are using Windows 3.1.

■ **Student Disks** Three blank disks (described in the Student Disks section, above)

■ **Course Labs and Local Page Files** See your instructor or technical resource person to obtain the two Course Labs and the local page files for Session 1.1 to put on your hard disk. You can also download the local page files from the Student Online Companion at **http://www.2.coursetools.com/cti/NewPerspectives/tiun/**.

VISIT OUR WORLD WIDE WEB SITE

Additional materials designed especially for you are available on the World Wide Web at the Online Companion of the Course Technology Student Center. Go to **http://coursetools.com**.

This book assumes that students are using Netscape Navigator 2.0. The screens in this book show Netscape Navigator running under Windows 95, but students running Netscape Navigator under Windows 3.1 will still be able to use the book successfully. Trouble? paragraphs throughout the book note differences students may see if they are using Windows 3.1.

STUDENT DISKS

To complete the tutorials in this book, your students must have three blank, formatted Student Disks, which they use to save and download files. They should label and use them according to the table in the To the Student section above.

LOCAL PAGE FILES

Students will also need access to the local page files that they open in Session 1.1. These files are provided on a CD-ROM that accompanies this text. Please see the Readme file for instructions on copying the local page files to your computer lab network. These files may also be downloaded from the Faculty and Student Online Companions on the World Wide Web. Once you have copied these files onto your network, students can use the Open File command to access the local site. *Be sure to tell students where to find these files if your network path is different from the one listed in Step 3 on page NS 17.*

THE COURSE TECHNOLOGY ONLINE COMPANIONS

Because the Internet is always changing, this book guides students to the Internet and World Wide Web via the Student Center site maintained by Course Technology. By having students use the Student Center, instead of having them access external URLs directly, we ensure that they will access live links, minimize the possibility of obsolete links, and give them a more successful Internet learning experience. For information on the Faculty Online Companion, see the Preface.

COURSE LABS

This book features two interactive Course Labs to help your students understand Internet World Wide Web and e-mail concepts. There are Lab Assignments at the end of Tutorials 1 and 3 that relate to these labs. The Lab software is distributed with the local page files on a CD-ROM and can be installed by following the setup instructions in the Readme file. Once you have installed the Course Labs software, your students can start the Labs using the instructions in the To the Student section above.

CTI SOFTWARE

You are granted a license to install the Course Labs and the local site file to any computer or computer network used by students who have purchased this book.

TUTORIAL 1

Navigating the Internet with Netscape

Conducting Teacher Workshops at Northern University

LAB

The Internet
World Wide Web

CASE

Northern University

Stephan Gord and Michelle Pine, education students at Northern University, are researching the use of the Internet as a teaching tool in the classroom and as an aid for preparing class lessons. Though from very different backgrounds, both students developed an interest in the Internet after using electronic mail (e-mail). Stephan is a European exchange student who keeps in contact with his academic advisors in England through Northern University's Internet connection. Michelle uses an online service at home to communicate with her family living in New Mexico.

Stephan and Michelle are amazed at the wealth and variety of information they found freely available on the Internet, especially the amount geared toward educators. At forums, educators can share ideas, advice, and encouragement. Teachers can find current information about every subject matter that can be incorporated into the curriculum. Geography and history, for example, come alive with multimedia travel through various time periods and lands. Science is no longer limited by physical equipment, and students can conduct experiments in virtual labs that would be impossible in many classrooms. Humanities become more vibrant through tours of world-famous museums, music, and video clips from particular artists, styles, or times. The more Michelle and Stephan looked, the more resources they found. What's more, they discovered that information is updated and added daily.

Next week, Stephan and Michelle are conducting a two-hour workshop for teachers on Internet basics and Netscape Navigator based on their research. The 25 educators enrolled in the workshop teach kindergarten to twelfth grade in the local public school district. The enrollees have little working knowledge of the Internet and Netscape Navigator but are interested in its possibilities.

To practice their presentation, Stephan and Michelle ask you to listen to parts of their talk and to help prepare the materials for the educators.

Using the Tutorials Effectively

These tutorials will help you learn about Netscape Navigator. They are designed to be used at a computer. Each tutorial is divided into sessions designed to be completed in about 45 minutes, but take as much time as you need. Watch for the session headings, such as Session 1.1 and Session 1.2. It's also a good idea to take a break between sessions.

Before you begin, read the following questions and answers, which are designed to help you use the tutorials effectively.

Where do I start?

Each tutorial begins with a case, which sets the scene and gives you background information to clarify what you will be doing in the tutorial. Ideally, you should read the case before you go to the lab. In the lab, begin with the first session.

How do I know what to do on the computer?

Each session contains steps that you will perform on a computer to learn how to use Netscape Navigator. Read the text that introduces each series of steps. The steps you need to do at a computer are numbered and set against a colored background. Read each step carefully and completely before you try it.

How do I know if I did the step correctly?

As you work, compare your computer screen with the corresponding figure in the tutorial. Don't worry if your screen display is somewhat different from the figure. The important parts of the screen display are labeled in each figure. Check to make sure these parts are on your screen.

What if I make a mistake?

Don't worry about making mistakes; they are part of the learning process. Paragraphs labeled "TROUBLE?" identify common problems and explain how to get back on track. Follow the steps in a TROUBLE? paragraph *only* if you are having the problem described. If you run into other problems:

- Carefully consider the current state of your system, the position of the pointer, and any messages on the screen.

- Complete the sentence, "Now I want to... ." Be specific, because you are identifying your goal.

- Develop a plan for accomplishing your goal, and put your plan into action.

How do I use the Reference Windows?

Reference Windows summarize the procedures you learn in the tutorial steps. Do not complete the actions in the Reference Windows when you are working through the tutorial. Instead, refer to the Reference Windows while you are working on the assignments at the end of the tutorial.

How can I test my understanding of the material I learned in the tutorial?

At the end of each session, answer the Quick Check questions. The answers for the Quick Checks are at the end of the tutorials.

After you have completed the entire tutorial, complete the Tutorial Assignments and Case Problems. They are carefully structured so you will review what you have learned and then apply your knowledge to new situations.

What if I can't remember how to do something?

Refer to the Task Reference at the end of the tutorials; it summarizes how to accomplish tasks using the mouse, the menus, and the keyboard.

Now that you've seen how to use the tutorials effectively, you are ready to begin.

Frequently Asked Questions (FAQs) about the Internet

When Stephan and Michelle started their project, they had a lot of questions about the Internet: what is it?, where is it?, whose is it?, and so on. They found that many people new to the Internet frequently ask the same questions. They decide to begin their presentation by answering these common questions.

What is the Internet and who created it?

The **Internet** is the largest and most widely used computer network in the world—a network of networks connected by fiber optic cables, satellites, phone lines and other communication systems. A **network** is two or more individually controlled computers that are connected so users can share data and resources such as a printer. Within each network, one computer is designated as the network **server**, a computer with special software and large file storage capabilities. Two or more connected networks form an **internetwork**, or internet, across which users can share information. For example, in Figure 1-1, the computers in Networks 1 and 2 can share information through their server connections, but not with Network 3, which is isolated from, or not connected to, the other networks.

Figure 1-1 ◀
Internetwork

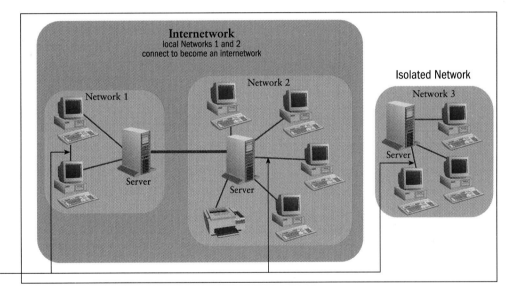

network connections

The Internet began in the 1960s when the U.S. Department of Defense was researching how to build a network of geographically dispersed computers that would continue to function even if one of the computers on the network failed to operate (such as in the case of a bomb attack). In 1969, the Advanced Research Projects Agency (ARPA), created by the Department of Defense, connected four computer networks to form an internetwork called ARPANET. The decentralized structure of ARPANET made it easy for other networks to connect to it. Gradually other government, academic, and industrial networks were added to the ARPANET and it became known as the Internet, or the **Net**.

Who owns and operates the Internet?

No single person, corporation, institution, or agency owns or operates the entire Internet, although individuals, private corporations, educational institutions, or government agencies own and operate each of the smaller networks that comprise the Internet.

On the Internet, there are no rules about where information is stored; all the data pertaining to a topic are rarely stored on one computer. Further, no one regulates or screens the data, so the quality of information varies. For these reasons, the Internet is often considered an electronic frontier, filled with adventure, change, and a wealth of knowledge.

In recent years, the Internet has come under scrutiny and groups have been formed to self-regulate the Internet rather than have the government impose regulations. The Electronic Frontier Foundation (EFF), established in 1990, addresses social and legal issues involving electronic distribution of information. It focuses on civil liberties and protection of the First Amendment right to freedom of speech as it applies to the electronic society of the Internet. The EFF is active in fighting government regulations and finding alternate ways to control the Internet. The Internet Society (ISOC), started in 1992, is an international organization that is trying to develop and implement standards for the Internet and its associated technologies. ISOC also maintains historical and statistical databases about Internet usage. As with any new frontier, the Internet will eventually become settled and a formal set of rules will evolve. Some of the early pioneers of the Internet might find the changes too confining, but the refinement of the Internet civilization will continue to occur.

How does the Internet work?

An Internet site, or **host**, is a network server that is connected to the Internet and permits people around the world to access its files. The Internet would be impossible if every host site on the globe needed to connect directly every other host in order to request information. Instead, local hosts can attach to a major connection (or communication link) called a **backbone**. Like a freeway that encourages high-speed travel and efficient movement, the backbone quickly moves information long distances and provides a cost-effective way to link local area networks (LANs) worldwide. Figure 1-2 shows a portion of the Internet structure.

Figure 1-2 ◀
Internet is
network of
networks

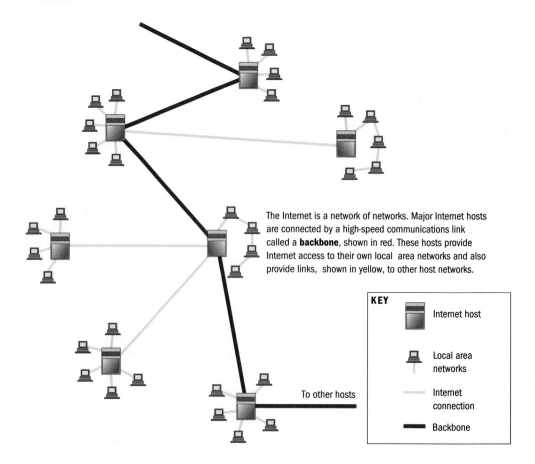

The Internet is a network of networks. Major Internet hosts are connected by a high-speed communications link called a **backbone**, shown in red. These hosts provide Internet access to their own local area networks and also provide links, shown in yellow, to other host networks.

To other hosts

KEY

▦	Internet host
▣	Local area networks
──	Internet connection
━━	Backbone

In the mid-1980s, hosts were clustered into groups (called **domains**) to make them easier to locate. Each domain is identified by a domain name similar to a family surname. Just as family members share a surname yet live in separate households both nearby and far away, a domain contains one or more hosts that might be at the same physical location or spread great distances apart. Some domains are small and contain just a few hosts. Others are very large and might contain 100 hosts. Examples of domains are an educational institution or a government agency.

What can you do on the Internet?

The Internet provides many services, which you can use to communicate with people around the world, to access and retrieve data, and to obtain software. The six services and their purposes are:

- **E-mail**. Send electronic messages to other users.

- **World Wide Web (WWW)**. Find and view information about a wide variety of topics.

- **FTP**. Transfer to and from your computer files of text, graphics, music, animations, or videos.

- **Telnet**. Run programs on a remote host, play interactive games, and use remote library card catalogs.

- **Gopher**. Search for documents, databases, and library card catalogs.

- **Usenet**. Participate in online discussion groups about a variety of topics.

You'll probably use some of these services more frequently than others. For example, many people begin using the Internet through e-mail and then branch out into other areas. You'll learn more about these services in these tutorials.

How big is the Internet?

The Internet began in 1969 with just four hosts, but today connects nearly 7 million hosts in 120,000 domains in 140 countries[1] with an estimated 20 to 30 million users[2]. Figure 1-3 shows a chart of the Internet's growth from 1969 to 1995.

---

[1]http://www.nw.com/zone/www/top.html, Networks Wizards
[2]http://www.mids.org/mids/about.html, Matrix Information and Directory Services

Figure 1-3 ◀
Internet growth

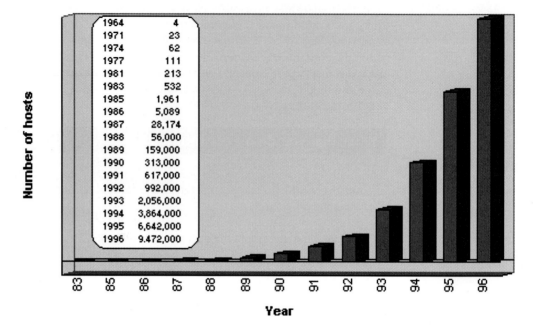

1964	4
1971	23
1974	62
1977	111
1981	213
1983	532
1985	1,961
1986	5,089
1987	28,174
1988	56,000
1989	159,000
1990	313,000
1991	617,000
1992	992,000
1993	2,056,000
1994	3,864,000
1995	6,642,000
1996	9,472,000

Though steadily increasing since its inception, the Internet surged in 1986 when the National Science Foundation (NSF) added the NSFNET (with five supercomputer centers) to the Internet and allowed universities access. The number of hosts increased by 450 percent in one year. The next growth spurt occurred in the late 1980s, when 17 foreign countries connected to the Internet. At that point, the Internet became a worldwide entity and ARPANET ceased to exist. The latest surge came in 1993 with the onset of the World Wide Web (WWW). Since then, the number of Web sites has doubled every three to five months, and as of early 1996, one in every 100 hosts on the Internet have Web servers[3]. If the growth trends continue, Web servers will soon dominate the Internet.

Are cyberspace and the information superhighway the same thing as the Internet?

Both terms—*cyberspace* and the *information superhighway*—are used to describe the Internet.

Science fiction writer William Gibson coined the term **cyberspace** in his 1984 novel, *Neuromancer*, to describe the imaginary place he envisioned behind the computer screen. His characters plugged their brains into the computer to prowl around great warehouses of data. By 1989, people were referring to the Internet as "cyberspace." Usually, however, cyberspace is used to describe a mystical world seen from the vantage point of a window (in this case, the computer screen).

The term **information superhighway** is a commonly used analogy for the Internet. The

---

[3]http://www.netgen.com/info, Matthew Gray

The term **information superhighway** is a commonly used analogy for the Internet. The worldwide network of computers linked by telephone lines, cables, microwaves, and satellites makes up the information superhighway. The towns on the highway are all the computers. The roads that connect the computers are fiber optic cables, satellites, and other communication systems. The cars that drive along the highway are the data—from advertisements to U.S. government documents—sent between the computers. Sometimes people apply the term *information superhighway* to only the physical connections between the computers on the network. More often, the term implies a busy world where work is continuously done by people sitting at computers.

Where do commercial information service providers fit into the picture?

A commercial information service provider, sometimes called an **online service provider,** offers subscribers access to its database of information and, sometimes, a connection to the Internet for a fee. These providers range from small neighborhood bulletin boards that run on a single microcomputer to large enterprises such as CompuServe, America Online, and Microsoft Network. The type and variety of services available depend on the provider, but they can include bulletin boards, electronic mail (e-mail), discussion or "chat" groups, and other ways of navigating the Internet. Like the networks that comprise the Internet, these services often compile their own databases of information, but unlike those on the Internet, they restrict data access to their members. They often control or approve the content available through them, so what subscribers access has been reviewed and accepted by that provider.

The World Wide Web

LAB

**The Internet
World Wide Web**

The **World Wide Web (WWW)** is an Internet service, which makes finding information and moving around the Internet easier. Although one of the newer Internet services, it has already become the most popular.

Before the WWW, a majority of the Internet consisted of text with few graphics and no sound. The Internet was difficult to use as well; you had to type out commands in order to locate information and move from one document to another. In 1989, Tim Berners-Lee, an information systems specialist at CERN (the European Laboratory for Particle Physics) in Geneva, Switzerland, realized the need to rapidly and easily link data between the growing number of databases on CERN's networks. He created the World Wide Web (commonly called the Web), which was released in 1992. The WWW is a global information-retrieval system based on the concept of a worldwide database of documents in which related information is linked by hypertext. **Hypertext** is a key word or phrase in a document that you select to link, or connect, to another related document. Hypertext is similar to a footnote except that you don't have to locate the referenced text and find the correct page; instead, the Web opens the referenced document when you click the hypertext. These documents, called **Web pages**, are files stored on Internet hosts throughout the world.

Hypermedia is hypertext that also contains links to multimedia, such as photographs, film clips, and sound, that make each document more attractive and fun to view as well as provides information not always available in text. Images and graphics also can be hypertext links that connect to other Web pages.

When you click a hypertext link, you are virtually jumping all around the world. One click can place you in Atlanta, another can put you in Australia, and the next can land you in Europe. Figure 1-4 shows a model of how the Web works.

Figure 1-4 ◄
How the
World Wide Web
works

1. Honolulu Community College (HCC), maintains an exhibit containing images, video clips, narration, and text about dinosaurs. Each image, video and document is a separate **page**, stored as a file on the HCC computer. You can jump from one page to another at HCC. For example, you can begin at the introductory screen, called a **home page**.

2. From the home page, you can jump to a page about iguanadons.

3. From this page you can jump to a page that contains a movie.

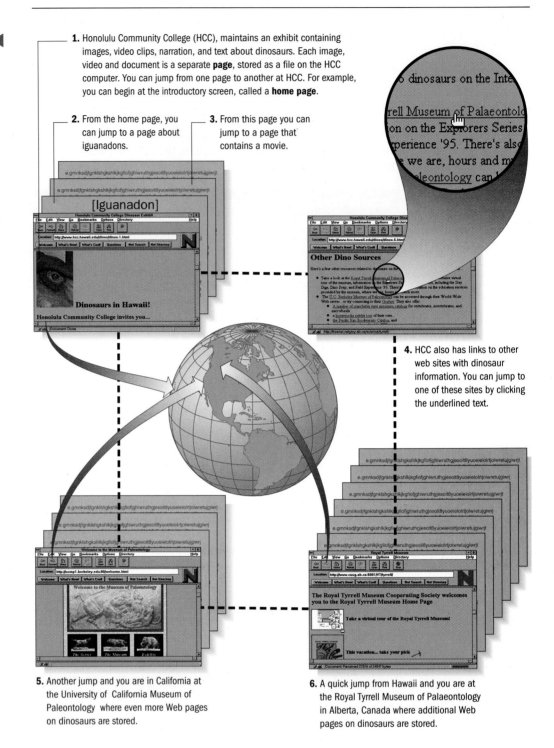

4. HCC also has links to other web sites with dinosaur information. You can jump to one of these sites by clicking the underlined text.

5. Another jump and you are in California at the University of California Museum of Paleontology where even more Web pages on dinosaurs are stored.

6. A quick jump from Hawaii and you are at the Royal Tyrrell Museum of Palaeontology in Alberta, Canada where additional Web pages on dinosaurs are stored.

What Is Netscape Navigator?

In order to access documents stored on Web servers, you need appropriate software, called a **Web browser**, which is a program that retrieves, interprets, and displays Web pages on your computer screen. **Netscape Navigator**, commonly called Netscape, is a powerful and easy-to-use Web browser capable of accessing Web documents, as well as any other type of Internet service. Netscape is the improved commercial version of **Mosaic**, the first graphical Web browser created in 1993 by undergraduate students at the University of Illinois at Urbana-Champaign.

Learning to use Netscape opens the door to almost the entire Internet. While navigating the Web, you can visit sites located around the world; view multimedia documents; download (transfer onto your computer) files, images, and sounds; send electronic messages (e-mail); conduct searches for specific topics; run software on other computers through Telnet, and get current news with Usenet. All these occur through one common interface—Netscape. Netscape handles all the commands and retrieval processes seamlessly, or transparently, so you need to learn only one software program to use most of the features on the Internet.

Putting It All Together

In short, the Internet is comprised of the computer networks that contain information and the physical connections between them. The WWW is a hypermedia information system that provides easy access to a large number of documents around the world. Netscape Navigator is a browser program you use to access and retrieve all the information on the Internet in a single, consistent way. Figure 1-5 shows how the Internet, WWW, and Netscape work together.

Figure 1-5 ◀
Putting it all
together

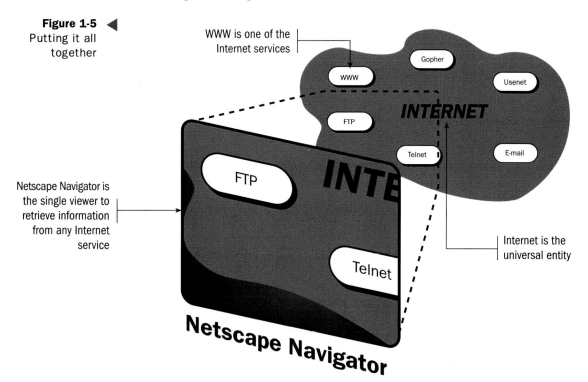

Netscape Navigator is
the single viewer to
retrieve information
from any Internet
service

SESSION

1.1

In this session, you will learn how to start and exit Netscape, identify components of the Netscape window, and initiate and abort a link.

Starting Netscape

Now that you know what the Internet, the WWW, and Netscape are and how they are related, you're ready to launch Netscape.

Michelle explains that, unlike many other software applications, Netscape does not always open with a standard start-up screen. A **home page** is the document you see when you first start Netscape, or another Web browser. (Some people also use the term *home page* to mean the first document that opens when you connect to another site.) A home page might include information about the host, links to other sites, or relevant graphics and sounds. Netscape allows each computer installation to specify what users will see when they start Netscape. When you launch Netscape, you might see:

- the Netscape home page

- your school's or institution's home page

- a page your technical support person sets as the default

- a blank page

When Michelle starts Netscape from home, she sees the Netscape home page. When she starts it in the university's lab, she sees Northern University's home page.

Netscape runs the same way, regardless of what operating system you are using, although the text and icons on the title bar vary slightly, depending on the operating system and version. The procedure for launching Netscape is the same as launching any other program on that system. If you are using a computer with Windows 95, start Netscape by following the steps in the next section, then skip to the section "The Netscape Window." If you are using a computer with Windows 3.1, skip the next set of steps and continue with the steps in the section "Launching Netscape from Windows 3.1."

Launching Netscape from Windows 95

You launch Netscape in Windows 95 just like you launch any other application. Note that, except for the figure in this section, the Windows 95 taskbar is not displayed in the figures throughout these tutorials.

To start Netscape from Windows 95:

1. If necessary, turn on your computer and get to the Windows 95 desktop.

2. Click the **Start** button ![Start] on the Windows 95 taskbar.

3. Move the mouse pointer over **Programs**. After a short pause, the Programs menu opens with a list of programs available on your computer.

    TROUBLE? If the Programs menu doesn't open and another menu does, repeat Step 3.

4. Move the mouse pointer over **Netscape** in the Programs menu, and then position the pointer over Netscape Navigator in the Netscape menu. See Figure 1-6.

Figure 1-6 ◀
Launching
Netscape
Navigator from
Windows 95

Figure 1-6 ◀
Launching
Netscape
Navigator from
Windows 95

move mouse pointer
here to open
Programs menu

Start button

move mouse pointer
here to open
Netscape menu

click to start
Netscape Navigator

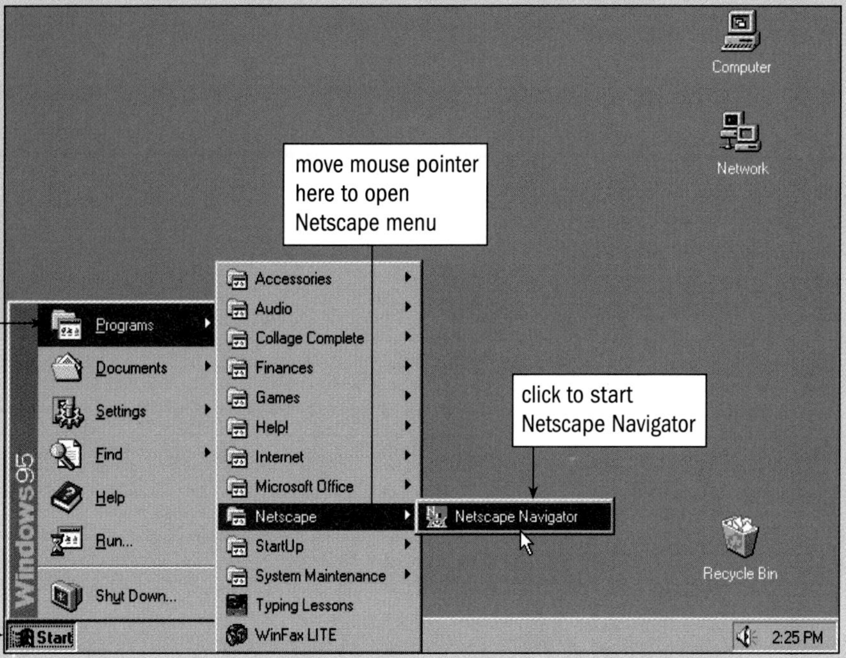

TROUBLE? If you don't see Netscape in the Programs menu, move the pointer over Netscape Navigator and click. If you still can't find Netscape or Netscape Navigator, ask your instructor or technical support person for assistance. If you are using your own computer, make sure Netscape is installed.

5. Click **Netscape Navigator** to start Netscape. The startup screen selected when Netscape was installed opens.

TROUBLE? If you're uncertain if you launched Netscape Navigator, check the title bar at the top of the window; it should contain "Netscape." If it doesn't, you might have selected the wrong icon. Click the File menu, then click Exit to close the program and return to the Windows 95 desktop. Repeat Steps 2 through 5.

6. Click the **Maximize** button 🗖 in the upper-right corner of the Netscape window if your Netscape window is not already maximized.

7. Skip the next section and continue with the section "The Netscape Window."

Launching Netscape from Windows 3.1

You launch Netscape in Windows 3.1 just like you launch any other application. The figures in these tutorials use Windows 95. Except for the title bar at the very top of the screen, everything else looks and works similarly, regardless of which version of Windows you are running.

To start Netscape from Windows 3.1:

1. If necessary, turn on your computer, make sure that Windows is launched and that the Program Manager window is open. You should see the Netscape group icon in the Program Manager window.

TROUBLE? If you don't see the Netscape group icon but you do see the Netscape icon, skip to Step 2. If you don't see either the Netscape group icon or the Netscape icon, ask your instructor or technical support person for assistance. The icon might have another name, or it might not be installed on your computer. If you are using your own computer, make sure Netscape is installed.

2. Double-click the **Netscape** group icon in the Program Manager window. The Netscape group window opens, and the Netscape icon appears within the Netscape group window. See Figure 1-7.

Figure 1-7 ◀
Launching
Netscape
Navigator from
Windows 3.1

Netscape group
window

click to start
Netscape Navigator

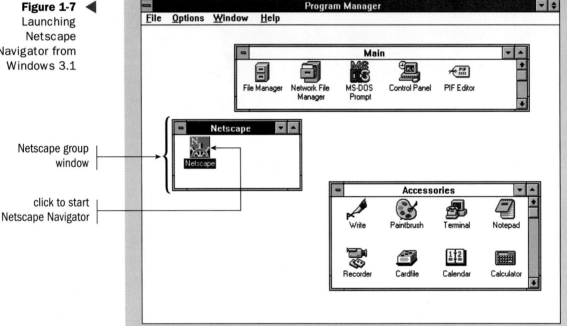

3. Double-click the **Netscape** icon. The startup screen selected when Netscape was installed opens.

TROUBLE? If you're not certain if you launched Netscape or another program, check the title bar at the top of the window; it should contain "Netscape." If it doesn't, you might have selected the wrong icon. Click the File menu, and then click Exit to close the program and return to the Program Manager window. Repeat Steps 2 and 3.

4. Click the **Maximize** button ▲ in the upper-right corner of the Netscape window if your Netscape window is not already maximized.

Components of Netscape Window

In most respects, the Netscape window looks and operates like other Windows programs, although it does contain a few additional features. One of the greatest advantages of using software that has a **graphical user interface** (GUI, pronounced gooey), such as Windows and Netscape, is that you don't have to relearn basic actions. The Netscape GUI uses a mouse pointer to click menus, buttons, icons, and other graphical symbols to perform specific operations just as Windows does. Figure 1-8 shows the Netscape window with the Netscape home page.

Figure 1-8
Components of
the Netscape
window

menu bar

toolbar

location box

directory buttons

page content area

status bar

title bar

Maximize button   Close button

status
indicator

pointer

vertical
scroll
bar

Title Bar and Menu Bar

The **title bar**, at the very top of the screen, identifies the active program and the name of the active Web page in brackets. The title bar on your screen should read "Netscape" followed by the name of the Web page you have open (in Figure 1-8, it's "Welcome to Netscape"). The **menu bar**, located directly below the title bar, accesses all the options available in Netscape. You can open a menu to see a list of commands grouped by category. For example, the File menu contains all the commands related to working with files. Many of the menu commands have keyboard shortcut equivalents or open up to reveal more choices.

Scroll Bars

You can use scroll bars to move around the page content area in Netscape just as you would to move around other Windows applications. The up and down arrows at the top and bottom of the **vertical scroll bar** move the page up or down. Sometimes, the content might not fit within the width of the content area. The left and right arrows on the **horizontal scroll bar** move the page from side to side. You can click the areas above or below the scroll box, click the scroll arrows, or drag the scroll box within the scroll bar to change the part of a page that is visible on your screen.

Toolbar

The **toolbar**, a band of graphical icons, is located beneath the menu bar. As with other Windows applications, the toolbar **buttons** provide shortcuts for some of the menu commands. Many people like to use toolbar buttons because they perform an action with a single click; although some people prefer to use the menu bar because each menu lists all the available commands. In this tutorial, you'll use the quickest and easiest method to perform an action.

Location Box

The **location box** appears immediately below the toolbar and shows the location or address of the current site you are visiting. Every site is identified by an address or path-name, called a **uniform resource locator** (URL), which tells Netscape where to find the site you want to visit. You'll learn more about URLs in the next session.

Directory Buttons

Directory buttons, located below the location box, are divided into categories that you can use to quickly find sites that contain information about a particular topic. Clicking each button opens a list of links related to that directory category. The links listed can change daily as information on the Internet changes. For example, when you click the What's New button, you'll see a list of links, each of which is followed by a short description of the site. Netscape Communications Corporation frequently updates the list of sites.

Status Bar and Indicator

The Netscape window also contains a status bar and a status indicator. At the bottom of the screen, the **status bar** shows your progress as you connect to a site; it also tells how large the document is and provides updates as to how much of the document is loaded into your computer's memory. The status bar is divided into three parts. The **security** icon indicates when a site is secure and you can safely send personal information to that site. The **status message area** displays a written message and the **progress bar** shows a color band that widens as information is transferred. The **status indicator**, the Netscape logo near the upper-right corner of your screen, animates as you connect to a site. Both the status bar and the status indicator advise you about where you are going and the progress of your request.

Setting Options for Netscape

Stephan asks you to look at a specific Web page. He was at that site earlier and saved it to a file so the educators attending the workshop will be able to get to it easily. You'll use the menu bar to open the file.

To open a file:

1. Position the pointer over the **File** menu and click. The menu opens, showing a list of commands related to working with files. See Figure 1-9.

Figure 1-9 ◀
File menu

click to open a file —

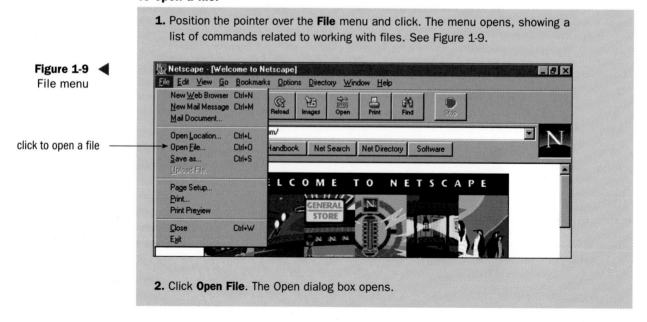

2. Click **Open File**. The Open dialog box opens.

3. Click in the File name text box, and then type **c:\nptiun\t1-1.htm** (or the filename supplied by your instructor for your lab setting) to indicate the location on the hard disk that Stephan stored the file. See Figure 1-10.

Figure 1-10 ◀
Open dialog box

type filename here ———

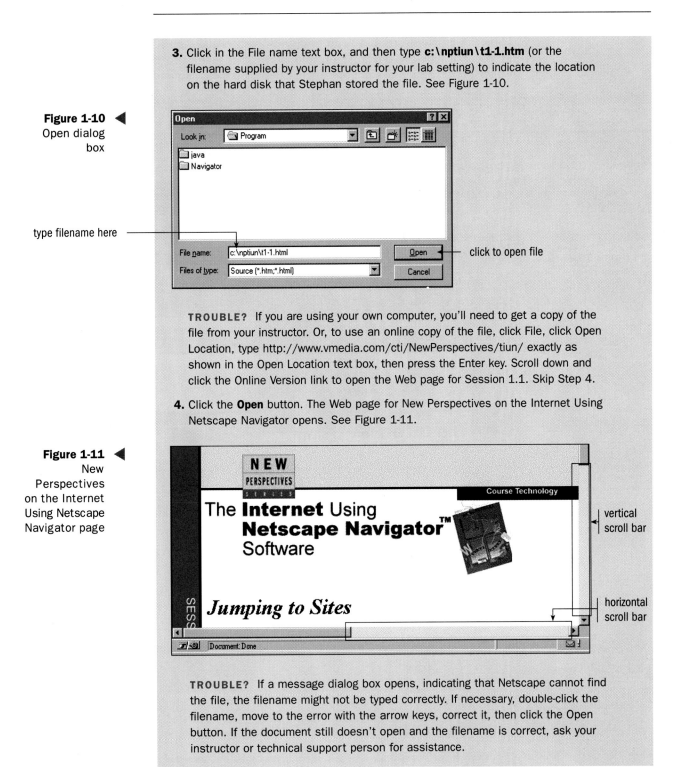

click to open file

TROUBLE? If you are using your own computer, you'll need to get a copy of the file from your instructor. Or, to use an online copy of the file, click File, click Open Location, type http://www.vmedia.com/cti/NewPerspectives/tiun/ exactly as shown in the Open Location text box, then press the Enter key. Scroll down and click the Online Version link to open the Web page for Session 1.1. Skip Step 4.

4. Click the **Open** button. The Web page for New Perspectives on the Internet Using Netscape Navigator opens. See Figure 1-11.

Figure 1-11 ◀
New Perspectives on the Internet Using Netscape Navigator page

vertical scroll bar

horizontal scroll bar

TROUBLE? If a message dialog box opens, indicating that Netscape cannot find the file, the filename might not be typed correctly. If necessary, double-click the filename, move to the error with the arrow keys, correct it, then click the Open button. If the document still doesn't open and the filename is correct, ask your instructor or technical support person for assistance.

Every time you start Netscape, make sure that you set up your screen to match the figures shown in the tutorials. For example, make sure that the toolbar, location box, and directory buttons are displayed. If you don't see one or more of these, you'll need to select the commands in the Options menu. The commands to show all these features are called **toggle switches** because they alternate between on and off, as a light switch does. You select the command once to turn on or show the feature and select it again to turn off or hide the feature.

Sometimes, you might not want to display every element on screen at once. For example, you can hide the directory buttons or another feature to enlarge the screen space available for the page content area. You can toggle the commands on or off at any time.

Right now, you want to make sure the Show Toolbar, Show Location, Show Directory Buttons and Auto Load Images commands in the Options menu are toggled on. You can tell if they are on just by looking at your screen; however, this time you'll also open the Options menu so you can toggle on any command that isn't already on.

To show or hide commands:

1. Click **Options** to open the Options menu. A check mark precedes any command that is toggled on. You should see a check mark before Show Toolbar, which indicates that the toolbar is toggled on and appears on the screen. See Figure 1-12.

Figure 1-12 ◀
Options menu

toggle on these
commands

click to save settings

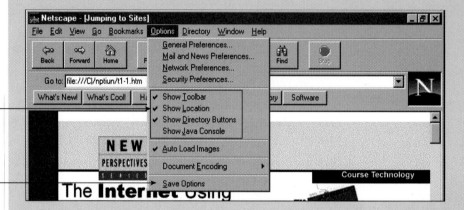

TROUBLE? If no check mark precedes the Show Toolbar command, then the toolbar is already hidden from view. Continue with Step 3.

2. Click **Show Toolbar** to remove the check mark and hide the toolbar. The toolbar disappears from view.

In these tutorials, you want the toolbar visible on the screen. You'll select the same command to toggle it on.

3. Click **Options**, and then click **Show Toolbar** again. The toolbar appears on the screen.

4. Repeat Steps 1 through 3 to make sure the Show Location, Show Directory Buttons, and Auto Load Images are toggled on. When you're finished, your screen should match Figure 1-12.

5. Click **Options**, and then click **Save Options** to save your settings. When you exit Netscape and restart it from the same computer, the toolbar and other features should toggle on automatically. If they don't, repeat these steps. If you use a different computer, make sure all these features are toggled on.

TROUBLE? If the Save Options command is dimmed (grayed out) or produces an error message when you click it, the command is not available for that computer. Each time you start Netscape, make sure all these commands are toggled on.

Viewing a Web Page Source File

Recall that any document available on a Web server is called a Web page. Because Web pages contain text and graphics and are designed with the visual elements in mind, they are often compared to magazine pages. Like a magazine page, a Web page can use a variety of font typefaces in different sizes and styles (for example, bold, italic, underlines). A Web page can be on a plain, colored, or other designed background similar to different types of paper quality, texture, and colors. Pictures or other graphics are usually part of both a magazine page and a Web page. Unlike a magazine page, however, a Web page might contain hypertext links in the text and graphics that bring you to a related Web page with a click of the button. Also, a Web page is neither constrained to a specific paper size nor affected by increasing costs of paper.

People who design Web pages use a simple coding system, called **HyperText Markup Language** (HTML), to format the contents of their pages. Similar to magazine typesetting code, HTML indicates which text should be formatted as headings, which text should be formatted as hypertext links, which text is a graphic, and so on. Netscape, or any other Web browser, decodes the HTML file and displays a Web page with the intended headings, links, graphics, and text. Anyone who creates a Web page must write and store the encoded HTML file, which is called a **source file**. You can view the source file for any Web page. Michelle suggests that you look at the source file for this page, which was specifically created by the publisher of these tutorials, Course Technology, Inc.

To view the HTML source for the current Web page:

1. Click **View** and then click **Document Source**. The HTML source file for the New Perspectives on the Internet Using Netscape Navigator page opens in a document window. See Figure 1-13. Notice the codes inside triangular brackets (< >). Each code instructs Netscape to display that content in a specific way.

Figure 1-13 ◀
Source File window

beginning of HTML source

indicates heading

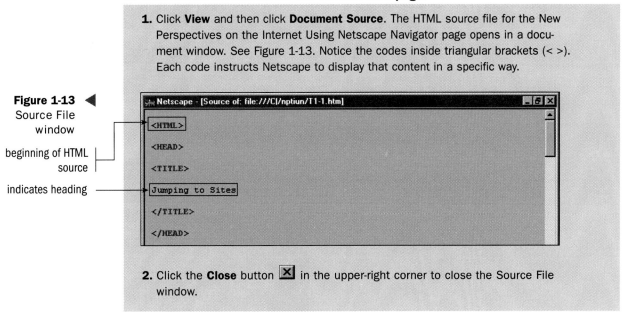

2. Click the **Close** button ⊠ in the upper-right corner to close the Source File window.

All source files for Web pages look similar to the one you just viewed. In addition to the title, headings, and text, the source file shows what sites you can link to from that page.

Linking to a Site

A hypertext **link** on the Internet, like a link in a chain, is a connector between two end points. You are looking at the New Perspectives on the Internet Using Netscape Navigator page, which contains several underlined hypertext phrases. Each is a set of directions that tell Netscape the path to follow in order to bring you to that site.

When you try to connect to another site, there are three possible outcomes. The connection can be successful, busy, or closed and abandoned. In a successful link, Netscape contacts the site (host) you want, connects into the site, transfers the data from the host to your computer, and displays the data on your screen. If many people try to link to a site simultaneously, the server might be busy and you can't get through. Sites that have been renamed or removed from the Internet are considered closed or abandoned.

The link might be completed so quickly that you don't have time to see all the internal steps, or it might be completed slowly. The amount of time it takes to connect to a site (or the **response time**) can vary, depending upon the number of people trying to connect to the same site, the number of people on the Internet at that time, and the site design.

Initiating a Link

Initiating a link starts a multi-step process. Fortunately, Netscape does the work for you. Still, it is important to follow the sequence of events so you can recognize problems when they occur and understand how to resolve them.

Figure 1-14 illustrates the string of events that occur when you link to a site. The first things you'll see when you begin a link is that the Stop button changes to red—its active state—and the status indicator animates. The status message area displays a series of messages indicating that Netscape has contacted the host (or site) you want to visit and is waiting for a reply, is transferring data, and finally, is done.

Figure 1-14 ◀
Watching the
status

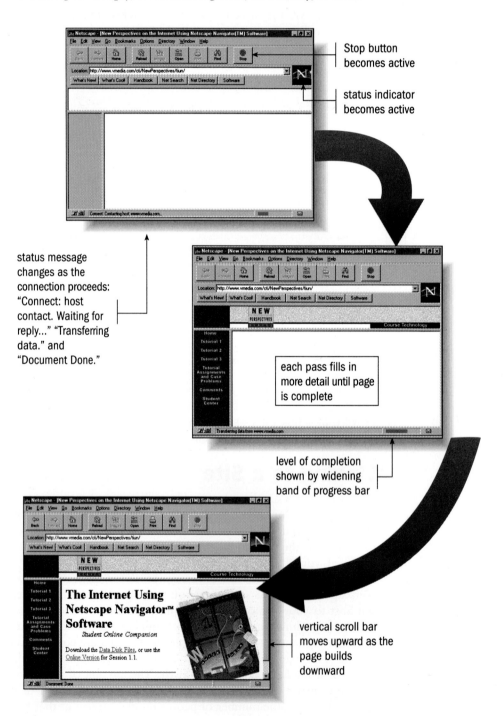

Stop button
becomes active

status indicator
becomes active

status message
changes as the
connection proceeds:
"Connect: host
contact. Waiting for
reply..." "Transferring
data." and
"Document Done."

each pass fills in
more detail until page
is complete

level of completion
shown by widening
band of progress bar

vertical scroll bar
moves upward as the
page builds
downward

You can see the Web page build as Netscape transfers information to your screen in multiple passes. The first wave brings a few pieces to the page and with each subsequent pass, Netscape fills in more detail until the material is complete. The progress bar fills in to indicate how much of the Web page has transferred. The vertical scroll box scrolls up as Netscape adds more information and detail to the page. You don't have to wait until the page is complete before scrolling or clicking another link, but it might be difficult to determine links and other information until the page is mostly filled in.

Stephan asks you to check that the site he wants to use to demonstrate a successful link is still current and easily accessible. He never had any trouble connecting to the site before and wants you to make sure it hasn't become more popular.

REFERENCE window

LINKING TO A WEB PAGE

- Place the pointer over a hypertext link.
- Make sure that the status message area displays a URL.
- Click the hypertext link.

To initiate a link to a Web page:

1. Scroll to the top of the New Perspectives on the Internet Using Netscape Navigator page.

2. Position your pointer on the **Successful site** link. Notice that the pointer changes shape from ⬐ to 🖑 indicating that you are pointing to a hypertext link, and that the status message area shows a URL (location address) for that link. See Figure 1-15.

   If the address you see in your status message area is not exactly the same as the one shown in Figure 1-15, don't worry. A site can rename its address just as easily as you can rename a file on a disk. Renaming happens quite often. Sometimes the changes are slight, and other times they are major.

Figure 1-15 ◀
Initiating a link

location address
(URL)

hypertext link

status message area

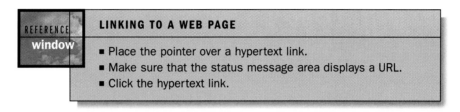

TROUBLE? If the status message area does not contain a URL, slowly move your pointer over the highlighted words. When you see a URL in the status message area, the pointer is positioned correctly.

3. Click the **Successful site** link to initiate the link. The status indicator animates, and the progress of the link is noted in the status bar. When the status message area reads "Document: Done," the link is complete and the Web page appears. See Figure 1-16.

Figure 1-16 ◀
Completed link

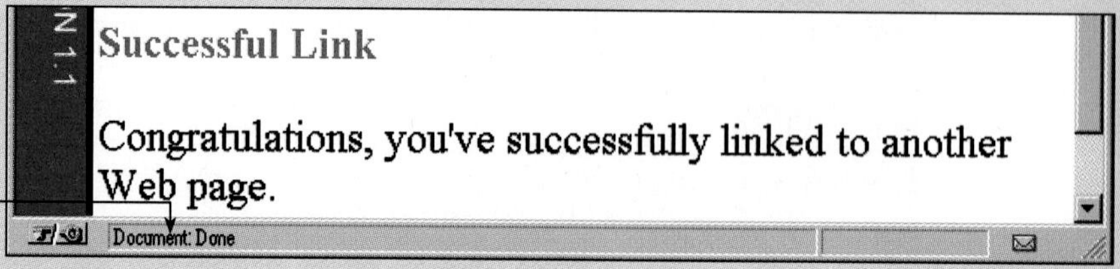

status message area ——————

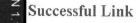

> **Successful Link**
>
> Congratulations, you've successfully linked to another Web page.
>
> Document: Done

TROUBLE? If a message dialog box opens, the link was not successful. Click the OK button to close the dialog box, and repeat Steps 3 and 4. After you click the hypertext link, make sure you do not click anywhere else on the page until the link is complete.

The link completed successfully. You are looking at a Web page that could be on a different computer in another country.

4. Click the **down arrow** on the vertical scroll bar to scroll down the Web page until you see another link.

5. Click the **Return to Session 1.1** link to return to that Web page.

You connected to a Web page with a single click, and then you used the hypertext link in that page to return to the New Perspectives on the Internet Using Netscape Navigator page. Using hypertext links is a simple way to move from one Web page to another.

Aborting a Link

Sometimes when you try to connect to a site, the link is not successful. Busy or abandoned sites and congestion are common problems on the Internet. Sometimes, sites become crowded and unavailable when many people try to access them at the same time. Other times, the number of people using the Internet is so heavy that it takes longer to travel between sites or is impossible to get there at all.

Much like an expressway, the Internet can become so congested that the paths cannot support the number of users at peak times. When this happens, traffic backs up and slows to a halt, in effect closing the road. At these peak times, the load is too heavy for the Internet. One solution is to go somewhere else because on this path, you won't go forward any time soon.

Aborting, or interrupting, a link is like taking the next exit ramp on the Internet. When the response time to a link seems too slow (longer than a few minutes) or nothing seems to be happening, you probably face a 15-minute or longer wait to complete the link. You can tell that a link is stalled when one of the following situations occurs:

- The status message area does not change, but
- the Stop button 🔲 on the toolbar is active, and
- the Netscape logo is animated.

Rather than waiting for a site that has a long queue or is so busy it can't even respond to your request, you can abort the link.

Stephan wants to show the workshop how to stop an unsuccessful link. There is one site that he has tried to visit many times but has been unsuccessful. He asks you to try to link to that site.

REFERENCE window	**ABORTING A LINK** ■ Click the Stop button to abort a stalled link. or ■ Click the OK button in the dialog box that appears to abort a link terminated by Netscape.

To abort a delayed link:

1. Scroll down until you see the Busy site link on the New Perspectives on the Internet Using Netscape Navigator page.

2. Click the **Busy site** link to initiate the link. Watch the status message area; it comes to a halt, although the status indicator remains animated and the Stop button active. The link is stalled. See Figure 1-17.

Figure 1-17 ◀
Stalled link

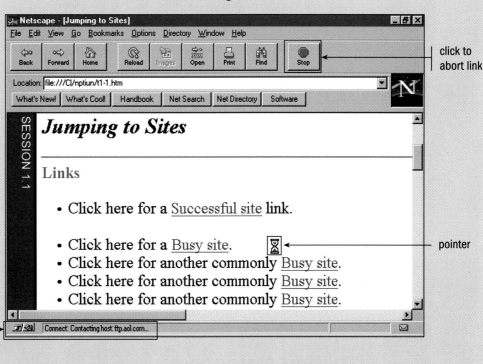

click to abort link

pointer

status message area doesn't change

TROUBLE? If the status message area reads "Document: Done" and a new Web page opens, you were able to connect to this site. Click the Back button on the toolbar and skip Step 3.

The line to visit this site might be very long, or many people might be using the Internet and you just can't get to the site. Either way, you'll want to abort the link rather than wait an interminable amount of time.

3. Click the **Stop** button on the toolbar to abort the link. The status indicator ceases to animate, and the Stop button dims.

Stephan plans to show the workshop that a link not only might complete successfully or stall, but that it might also be aborted by Netscape. He explains that Netscape terminates a link and displays an error message indicating the site was not found because:

- The URL specified by the hypertext link might no longer be active.

- The URL might be typed incorrectly.

- The server could not reach the site within the server's programmed wait time (for example, 90 seconds).

This message dialog box is the visual equivalent of the recorded telephone message, "If you'd like to make a call, please hang up and dial again." that you hear when you dial a number incorrectly or delay too long before dialing the entire number.

To end a Netscape terminated link:

1. If necessary, scroll down the page, and then click the **Closed or abandoned Internet site** link to initiate a link to a nonexistent or unanswered site. A message dialog box opens. See Figure 1-18.

Figure 1-18 ◀
Terminated link

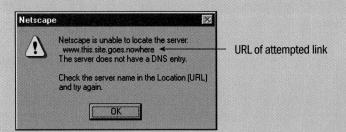

URL of attempted link

The dialog box indicates Netscape aborted the link because the URL is incorrect or no longer exists, or because the server does not have a domain name. Remember that every host site is part of a domain, or group, which has a name that usually begins "www." Each host can have a domain name registered with the Domain Name Server (DNS). When you link to a site, Netscape checks to see if the domain in its URL is registered with the DNS. If the site is not registered (similar to an unlisted telephone number in the phone book), Netscape opens the message dialog box. Unless you know the complete URL for that site, you cannot link to it.

2. Click the **OK** button to close the dialog box.

You have checked several of the sites Michelle and Stephan want to use in their workshop, and so far everything works just like they want it to.

Exiting Netscape

Michelle and Stephan decide to take a break and ask you to join them. Before you leave your computer, you need to close Netscape.

You can exit Netscape from any Web page, and unlike other programs, you don't need to save a document, file, or worksheet. Netscape does not store the Web pages currently on your screen. The next time you start Netscape, the window will show the home page designated for your installation, and you will need to link to those sites again if you want to see them.

To exit Netscape:

1. Click **File**.

2. Click **Exit**. The Netscape window closes.

You have completed Session 1.1. You have set options for Netscape, linked to a site successfully, aborted a stalled link, and had Netscape terminate a link for you.

Quick Check

1 True or False: When you start Netscape, you will always see the same screen, no matter what computer you are using.

2 What is a home page?

3 True or False: The directory buttons are found in the location box.

4 The _____ is the address of a Web site.

5 Clicking hypertext on the Web page initiates a _____.

6 Two Netscape components that show the progress and status of a link are the _____ and the _____.

7 When a link is complete, the message "_____" appears in the status message area.

8 When you link to a Web site, you might need to _____ the link because of congestion on the Internet.

SESSION 1.2

In this session, you will learn more about URLs, how to navigate the Internet with Netscape using toolbar buttons, how to print and e-mail Web pages, and how to use the online Help feature.

Opening a Location with a URL

Stephan and Michelle ask you to come to the workshop and help out. They want to show the instructors how to move around Web pages, where to find Internet resources, and how to use them in their classes. They ask you to help the instructors find the information they want.

Some of the educators mention that they've read journal articles about integrating the Internet into the curricula for all age groups. These articles usually supply Internet addresses for helpful online resources. Michelle explains how to access these sites.

Clicking a hypertext link is just one way of jumping to a Web page. These embedded links are an easy way to navigate the Internet when you don't have a specific destination in mind and just want to follow content links. Often, however, you'll want to visit a particular site. In order to get to that site, you need to know its address, which must be in a certain form, as you learned earlier. Entering the uniform resource locator (URL) for a Web page is a more direct route to get to a specific site.

A URL is composed of a protocol identifier, a server address, and a file pathname. For example:

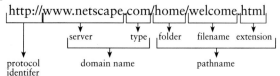

Computers use standardized procedures, called **protocols**, to transmit files. WWW documents travel between sites using **HyperText Transfer Protocol** (HTTP); so every URL for a Web page begins with "http://" to identify its type. Other protocols used on the Internet are File Transfer Protocol (FTP), news, and Gopher.

A **domain name** tells the exact location of the Internet server and the type of organization that owns and operates it. For example, in the domain name "www.netscape.com," the "www" indicates that the server is on the WWW, "netscape" indicates the name of the organization that owns the server, and ".com" indicates that it's a commercial-type site. The entire domain name means that Netscape is a commercial-type server on the WWW. Similarly, the domain name "www.nmu.edu" indicates that NMU is an educational-type server on the WWW. Other types of sites include organization (.org) and government (.gov). Outside the United States, domain name types include a two-letter country code. For example, .fi indicates that the server is located in Finland.

Finally, all files stored on a network server must have a unique pathname just as files on a disk do. The **pathname** includes the folder or folders the file is stored in plus the filename and its extension. The filename and extension is always the last item in the pathname. The filename extension for all Web pages is ".html," which stands for hypertext markup language. The URL "http://www.netscape.com/home/welcome.html" tells you that the hypertext markup language file "welcome" is located in a folder called "home" on the Netscape server, which is a commercial-type site on the Web.

Sometimes when you try to go to a specific site, you might see an error message such as the one shown in Figure 1-19. If you see an error message, you should check the URL in the location box and make sure every character is typed correctly, and then try again.

Figure 1-19 ◄
URL Not Found
error message

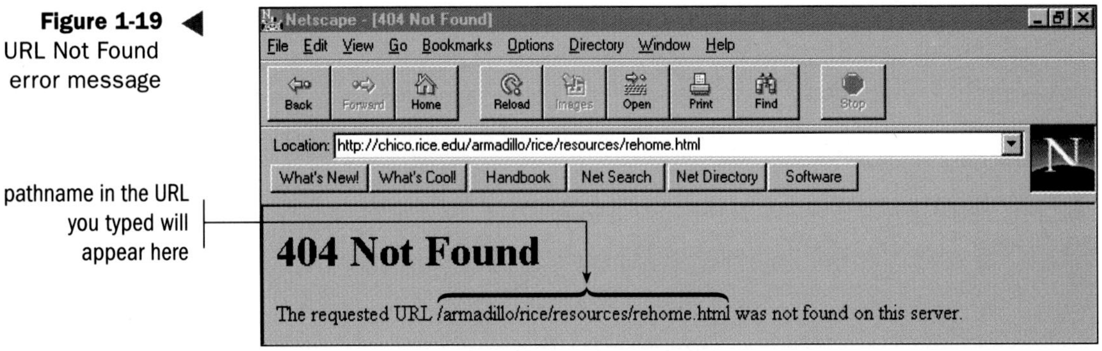

pathname in the URL
you typed will
appear here

404 Not Found

The requested URL /armadillo/rice/resources/rehome.html was not found on this server.

Remembering two important facts about a URL will make it significantly easier to use a URL to access an Internet site:

- **Domain names in a URL are case-sensitive.** A URL *must* be typed with the same capitalization shown. The URL http://www.Mysite.com is different from http://WWW.mysite.com. Unless the server can interpret case-sensitive addresses, you will get Netscape's error message when a URL doesn't exist with the exact name and capitalization entered. *Whether you copy a URL from a magazine article or get it from a friend, make sure you copy the characters and their cases exactly.*

- **Internet sites continuously undergo name and address changes.** A network server might have changed names, the file might be stored under a different directory, or the page you want might no longer be available. Remember, no one person or organization controls the Internet. Organizations and individuals can add files, rename them, and delete them at will. Often when a URL changes, you can find the forwarding address (URL) at the "old" URL. Other times, a site will simply vanish from a server, with no forwarding information.

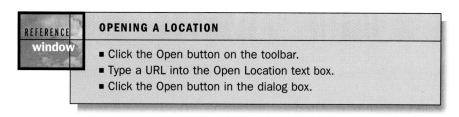

OPENING A LOCATION

- Click the Open button on the toolbar.
- Type a URL into the Open Location text box.
- Click the Open button in the dialog box.

Lyle Sanchez, one of the educators, wants to find a site he can bring his students as an in-class field trip. He asks you to help him.

To open a location:

1. Start Netscape and make sure the Show Toolbar, Show Location, Show Directory buttons, and Auto Load Images options are toggled on.

   TROUBLE? If you need help starting Netscape or setting the options, refer to the sections "Starting Netscape" or "Setting Options for Netscape."

2. Click the **Open** button [icon] on the toolbar to open the Open Location dialog box.

   The $\mathcal{I}$ is in the Open Location text box. This is where you type the URL of the site you want to access.

3. Type **http://www.vmedia.com/cti/NewPerspectives/tiun** into the text box. Make sure you type the URL exactly as shown. Notice the two slashes after the protocol identifier; the protocol identifier is always followed by the two slashes. See Figure 1-20.

Figure 1-20 ◄
Open Location
dialog box

type URL here ———

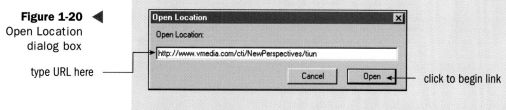

——— click to begin link

4. Click the **Open** button in the Open Location dialog box to open that site. Netscape follows the same steps as when you clicked hypertext to link to a site and connects to the selected Web page. See Figure 1-21.

Figure 1-21 ◄
Opened Web
page

URL of current
Web page

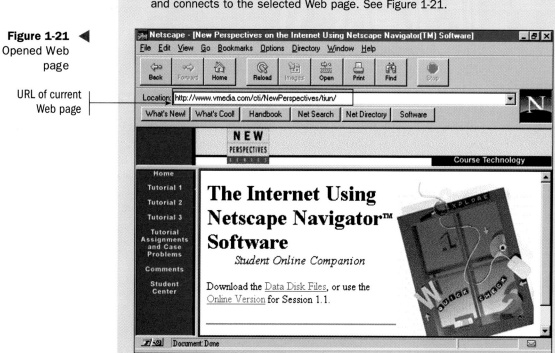

TROUBLE? If you receive a Not Found error message, the URL might not be typed correctly. Repeat Steps 2 through 4, making sure that the URL in the Open Location text box matches the one shown in Figure 1-20. Double-click in the Location text box, use the arrow keys to move to the error, and then make the correction. If the URL matches Figure 1-20 exactly, or if you see a different error message, press the Enter key to try connecting to the Web page again. If you see the same error message, ask your instructor or technical support person for help.

5. Click the **Tutorial 1** link in the band on the left side of the Web page to open the Learning to Navigate page.

This Web page contains hypertext links to other educational resource sites available on the Internet. Lyle wants to look at the Field Trips/Museums link.

6. Click the **Field Trips/Museums** link in the Subject Areas list to see the list of sites available from this Web page. See Figure 1-22.

Figure 1-22 ◄
Field
Trips/Museums
list

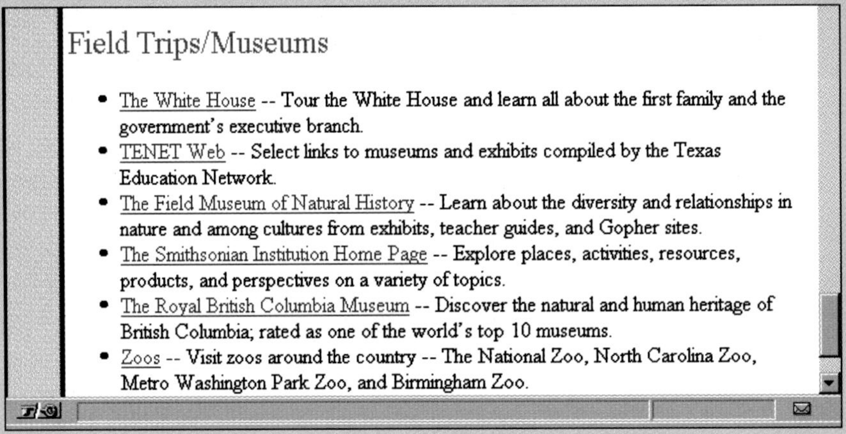

Field Trips/Museums

- The White House -- Tour the White House and learn all about the first family and the government's executive branch.
- TENET Web -- Select links to museums and exhibits compiled by the Texas Education Network.
- The Field Museum of Natural History -- Learn about the diversity and relationships in nature and among cultures from exhibits, teacher guides, and Gopher sites.
- The Smithsonian Institution Home Page -- Explore places, activities, resources, products, and perspectives on a variety of topics.
- The Royal British Columbia Museum -- Discover the natural and human heritage of British Columbia; rated as one of the world's top 10 museums.
- Zoos -- Visit zoos around the country -- The National Zoo, North Carolina Zoo, Metro Washington Park Zoo, and Birmingham Zoo.

Lyle looks at some of the places a teacher and students could explore on the WWW. Although they cannot physically go to these places, with a computer and the Internet, they can still make use of the resources at that location.

Lyle wants to know how he can use hypertext links and URLs to go back to the Web pages he's just visited so he can try different links. Stephan tells him that Netscape provides an easier way to move among the Web pages he's already visited.

Moving among Web Pages

In Netscape, you can flip among open Web pages as though they were pages in a magazine that you have held with a finger. Rather than memorizing and retyping URLs of places you have visited, you can use toolbar buttons to move back one page at a time through the pages, move forward again one page at a time, or return to the "front cover" of your home page.

You'll show Lyle how to move around the Web pages Stephan and Michelle have had the workshop visit.

To move among visited Web pages:

1. Look at the Forward button ⊡ on the toolbar. It is dimmed because you are at the latest page you have viewed since starting Netscape. However, the Back button ⊡ on the toolbar is active, indicating that you have looked at other Web pages. See Figure 1-23.

button dimmed,
indicating latest page

Figure 1-23 ◀
Netscape
toolbar

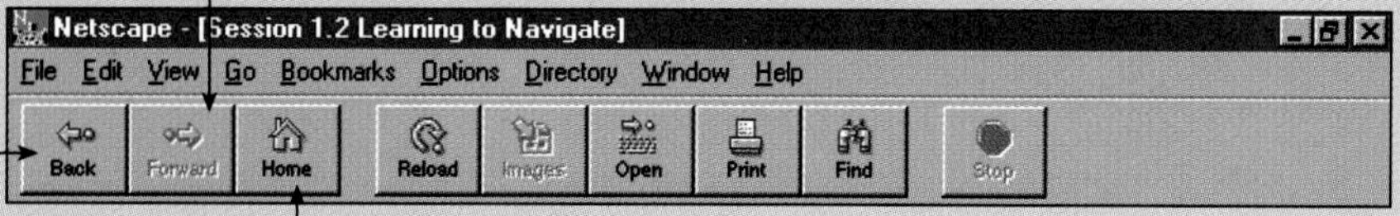

click to return to
previous Web page

click to return to
home page

2. Click ⊡. The Learning to Navigate page reappears on your screen.

3. Click ⊡ until you return to your home page. Notice that the Back button dims, indicating that you reached the first page you viewed since you started Netscape; you can move back only as far as the home page.

   TROUBLE? If your Back button is already dimmed after you return to the Learning to Navigate page, then you are at *your* starting point, and your Netscape installation does not have a home page that appears upon startup. Just continue with Step 4.

   You have moved backward through the earlier pages and now can return to the latest site you visited, the Field Trips/Museums list. The Forward button, like the Back button, moves you one page at a time.

4. Click ⊡ until you see the Field Trips/Museums list. Notice that the Forward button is dimmed again, indicating that you are looking at the last page you visited.

   TROUBLE? If your Forward button is *not* dimmed, you have linked from the Learning to Navigate page to another Web page. Continue clicking the Forward button ⊡ until it is dimmed; this is *your* furthest point of travel.

   Your home page usually contains familiar information and resources, so you frequently want to return there. Netscape provides a way to get back to your home page with a single click—the Home button.

5. Click the **Home** button ⊡ on the toolbar to return to your home page.

   TROUBLE? If the Home button is dimmed, your Netscape installation does not designate a home page location and the initial page content area when you started Netscape was blank. Just continue with the tutorial.

You've seen that it's simple to navigate through Web pages, but sometimes the pages take quite a while to load. Michelle tells the workshop participants that pages load more quickly when they don't contain images.

Loading Images

Images, the graphics and pictures such as drawings or photographs that accompany a Web page, make Internet documents more attractive and informative and can enhance comprehension. For example, if you're studying modern history, you can find up-to-date information on the Internet about the geography and current events of warring countries. Because the countries' borders change so quickly, maps that accompany these articles are more current than any printed atlas.

However, the use of graphics significantly increases the time a Web page takes to load. A page that contains only text loads in seconds whereas one containing elaborate images can take minutes. Clearly, a trade-off exists between speed and quality. Deciding which factor to favor depends on the situation. When you have a lot of time or enjoy the richness of images, you might want to automatically load the images for every page. When you want to look at a large number of pages in a short amount of time, you probably want to load images selectively. With Netscape, you can switch between these two options as frequently as you want. You can determine easily if the Auto Load feature is set by looking at the Web page on your screen. If you see **icons**, small square representations of images, rather than the complete images, then the feature is turned off. But not every Web page includes images; so if you don't see either icons or images, you'll need to examine the toolbar.

If the Image button is dimmed, as it is on your screen now, you are set to Auto Load Images. Although the reverse might seem to be the case, the button is active only when you are set to load images on demand for a specific Web page. If you are loading images automatically, you don't need the button and it is dimmed. Netscape's default is set to Auto Load Images.

Viewing Images on Demand

You might opt for speed and load images only when you really want or need to see them. In such cases, any image on a Web page is represented with an icon similar to 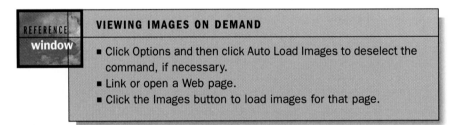. Although this option offers speed, the advantage of loading images automatically is that you can see and use all the links that are on the page. Remember that images also can be links to other Web pages. Unless you load the images, you won't be able to use or even see these links.

Stephan and Michelle ask you to find sites that the teachers might want to use in their classes. You'll view the next pages without graphics so that they will load faster.

REFERENCE window	**VIEWING IMAGES ON DEMAND**
	■ Click Options and then click Auto Load Images to deselect the command, if necessary. ■ Link or open a Web page. ■ Click the Images button to load images for that page.

To view Web pages without images:

1. Click **Options** to open the menu. A check mark appears in front of Auto Load Images to indicate that it is active. Now toggle off the command so that images don't load automatically.

2. Click **Auto Load Images** to toggle off the command. The Options menu closes and the Images button on the toolbar is active, so you can click it when you want to load images.

3. Click the **Back** button to return to the Learning to Navigate page.

   Although you toggled off the Auto Load Images command, the image still appears on the page. This happens because you loaded images automatically when you first connected to the Learning to Navigate page. When you requested the link again, you merely retrieved the copy from your computer's memory with the images already loaded.

4. Click the **Field Trips/Museums** link, then click the **Zoos** link to open the Zoos page, which contains links to several national zoos. Notice that icons replace the images. See Figure 1-24.

Figure 1-24 ◀
Zoos page with
image icons

icons replace images

more text fits on page

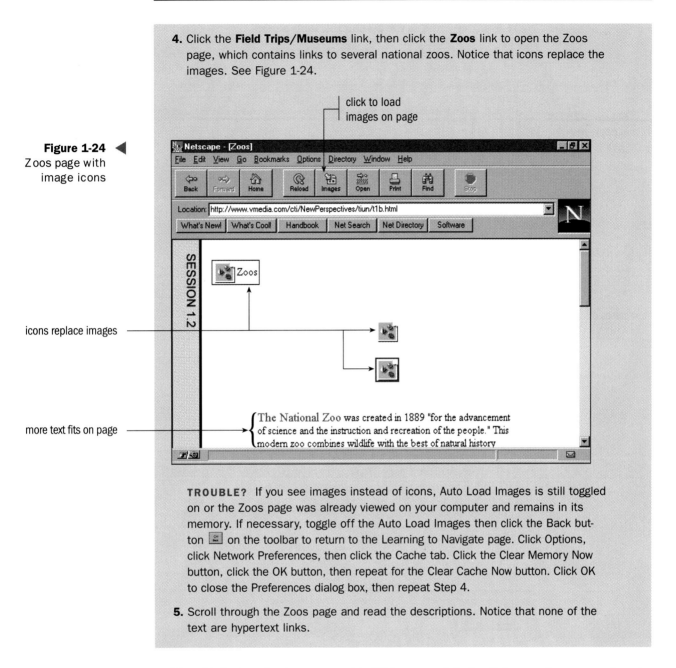

TROUBLE? If you see images instead of icons, Auto Load Images is still toggled on or the Zoos page was already viewed on your computer and remains in its memory. If necessary, toggle off the Auto Load Images then click the Back button 🔳 on the toolbar to return to the Learning to Navigate page. Click Options, click Network Preferences, then click the Cache tab. Click the Clear Memory Now button, click the OK button, then repeat for the Clear Cache Now button. Click OK to close the Preferences dialog box, then repeat Step 4.

5. Scroll through the Zoos page and read the descriptions. Notice that none of the text are hypertext links.

You think that the images on this Web page might be links to other pages that the teachers might want to see because none of the text contain links. You decide to load the images to see all your link options.

To load the images for a selected Web page:

1. Click the **Images** button on the toolbar to replace the icons with images. The page reloads from top to bottom with the images. When it's completely loaded, your page should look like Figure 1-25.

Figure 1-25 ◀
Zoos page with
images loaded

images replace icons ⟶

text scrolls off screen ⟶

The page is much more interesting to view this way and contains other links you couldn't see with the icons.

2. Click a zoo image to link to that zoo's Web page.

3. Click [Images] to load the images for this page.

Everyone in the workshop is amazed at the clarity of the photographs and the richness of the page. They agree that these types of resources would encourage students to investigate subjects more thoroughly.

4. Click **Options**, and then click **Auto Load Images** to set images to load automatically. Now any other Web page you visit will load with the images.

USES AND abuses

EDUCATIONAL USES

The Internet provides many ways to enhance learning and provide more educational opportunities to students:

- distance learning (for example, reaching rural areas with specialized courses)
- school and classroom home pages to publish student projects and yearbooks
- virtual field trips for the sciences and humanities
- independent, self-paced learning opportunities
- career planning and academic advising

Previewing and Printing a Web Page

Although reducing paper consumption is an advantage of browsing information online, sometimes you'll find it useful to print a Web page. For example, you might want to refer to the information later when you don't have computer access, or you might want to give a copy of the Web page to someone who doesn't have access to a computer or to the Internet.

You should always preview a Web page before you print it. Although Web pages can be any size, printers tend to use 8½ × 11-inch sheets of paper. When you print, Netscape automatically reformats the text of the Web page to fit the page dimension. Because lines might break at different places or text size might be altered, the printed Web page might be longer than you expect.

You decide that the directory of zoos is a good handout for the teachers in the workshop, so you decide to print out a copy. First, you'll preview it to see how many pages the Web page will print on and that it appears on the printed page as you expect.

To preview a Web page:

1. Click the **Back** button [image] on the toolbar until you see the Zoos page.

2. Click **File**, and then click **Print Preview**. The Print Preview window opens with the first page of the Web page displayed. See Figure 1-26.

Figure 1-26 ◄
Print Preview of
Zoos page

click to send page
to printer

click to see next page

header

footer

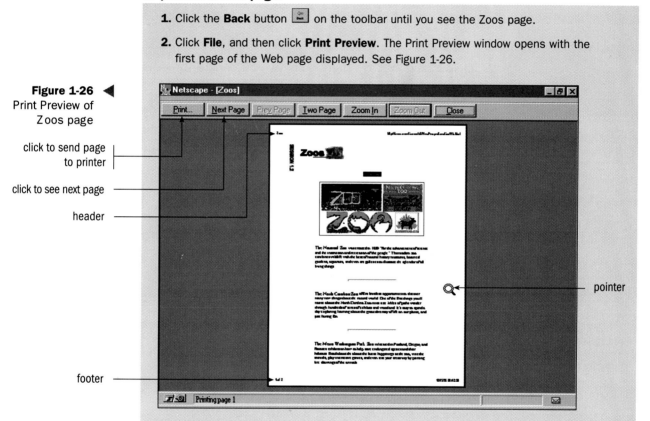

pointer

TROUBLE? If you see two pages on your screen, click the One Page button on the Print Preview toolbar.

The pointer shape changes to 🔍. You can click this pointer anywhere on the document to zoom it to a larger size.

3. Click 🔍 on the image at the top of the page to make it larger. Notice that the name of the Web page prints in the upper-left corner of the screen and the URL for that Web page prints in the upper-right corner of the screen.

Text that prints at the top of the page is called a **header**. Netscape prints a header on every page so you always know where to find that Web page on the Internet.

4. Click the **down arrow** on the vertical scroll bar to move to the bottom of the page and look at the page number in the lower-left corner of the page and the date and time in the lower-right corner of the page.

Text that prints at the bottom of the page is called a **footer**. Netscape prints a footer on every page so you can tell how many pages are in your document and when you printed it.

> **TROUBLE?** If you do not see headers or footers, your installation of Netscape might be set up differently. Just continue with Step 5.
>
> 5. Click 🔍 twice. The page returns to its original size.
>
> 6. Click the **Next Page** button on the Print Preview toolbar to see the material that didn't fit on the first page. Notice that Netscape automatically reformats the Web page into sections that fit on letter-sized sheets of paper.
>
> 7. Click the **Prev Page** button on the Print Preview toolbar to return to page one.
>
> 8. Click the **Two Page** button on the Print Preview toolbar to view the pages side by side.

This Web page is fairly short (only two 8½ × 11-inch sheets of paper). Other Web pages might convert to 30 or more 8½ × 11-inch sheets of paper, which might be longer than you need or want to print. You can use the Print command to print only those pages of which you want a hardcopy.

Although this Web page is only two sheets of paper, Michelle suggests that you print just the first page for the teachers. If the teachers want other information, they can return to the site and see the material online.

To print a Web page:

> 1. Click the **Print** button on the Print Preview toolbar to open the Print dialog box.
>
> 2. Click the **Pages** radio button, type **1** in the From text box, press the **Tab** key to move to the To text box, and then type **1**. This indicates that you want to print only the page range 1–1 of the document, or just the first page of the document. Your completed dialog box should look similar to Figure 1-27.

Figure 1-27 ◀
Print dialog box

your printer might
be different

select page range
to print

click to print

default is one copy

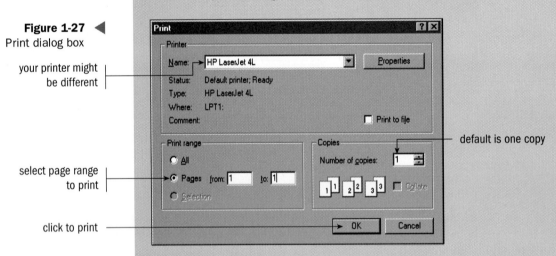

> **TROUBLE?** If your Print dialog box looks somewhat different from Figure 1-27, don't worry. The Print dialog box changes to reflect the options available for the printer you are using. Just continue with Step 3.
>
> 3. Click the **OK** button to print the first page of the Web page.

Several instructors in the workshop see Web pages that contain information they want to use or share with a colleague. Several have asked Stephan if they can print other pages to take with them. Michelle suggests that instead of printing the Web pages, they attach the page to an e-mail. This way, the printer won't be overloaded and everyone will be able to get the Web pages they want.

Attaching Web Pages to E-mail

An e-mail (electronic mail) message is a note or letter you write and send across the Internet. Unlike traditional mail that you send through the post office, e-mail is delivered almost immediately and conserves paper because you decide which messages, if any, to print. Sometimes, you'll want to add an attachment to your message. An **attachment** is a document you send with your e-mail message but that is not included in the body of the message. Just as you paper clip a note to a report or other document, you send an attachment with your e-mail message. Attachments can include documents from other programs, such as word-processing files, spreadsheets, and graphics, or Web pages.

Many times while using the Internet, you'll see a Web page you want to send in part or in whole to yourself if you're not on your own computer or to another person. The text content will transfer reliably if you attach it to an e-mail. If you want to keep the sophisticated formats and images, you can attach a Web page as an HTML source file. However, an HTML source file is difficult to read if the recipient doesn't have the proper converters installed on his or her computer.

You'll attach the Web page to e-mail and convert the Web page to text only. This way, the instructors can view the material with any word-processing program, and they won't need a Web browser to read the file.

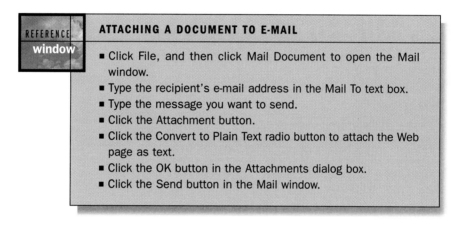

REFERENCE window

ATTACHING A DOCUMENT TO E-MAIL

- Click File, and then click Mail Document to open the Mail window.
- Type the recipient's e-mail address in the Mail To text box.
- Type the message you want to send.
- Click the Attachment button.
- Click the Convert to Plain Text radio button to attach the Web page as text.
- Click the OK button in the Attachments dialog box.
- Click the Send button in the Mail window.

To e-mail a document attachment:

1. Click **File**, and then click **Mail Document** to open the Mail Window. See Figure 1-28.

Figure 1-28 ◀
Mail window

click to mail message ──────

enter recipient's
e-mail address here

click to attach
Web page

type message here ──────

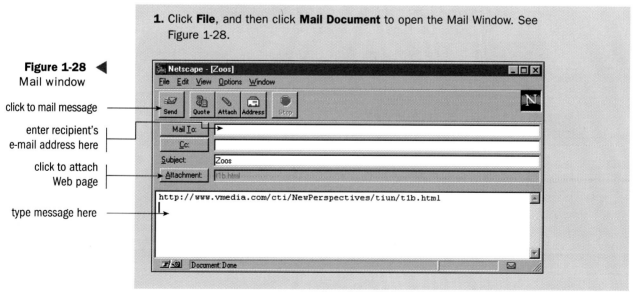

TROUBLE? If a message dialog box opens indicating "Your email address has not been specified. Before sending mail or news messages, you must specify a return address in Mail and News References," you need to enter your e-mail address. Click Options, click Mail and News Reference, click the Identity tab, type your e-mail address in the Your Email text box (for example, jdoe@nu.edu), then click the OK button. Repeat Step 1.

2. Type your full e-mail address in the Mail To text box.

   TROUBLE? If you don't know your full e-mail address, ask your instructor or technical support person for help.

3. Click in the message content box before the URL that is listed, and then type **I have attached an interesting Web page to this e-mail that I want to look at again later. It's URL is:**

4. Click the **Attachment** button to open the Attachments dialog box.

5. Click the **Attach Location (URL)** button to enter the URL of the current Web page. Notice that Netscape automatically uses the URL of the current Web page. Click the **OK** button, then click the **Convert to Plain Text** radio button to send the Web page as text rather than as the HTML source file. See Figure 1-29.

Figure 1-29 ◀
Attachments
dialog box

click to attach URL of
Web page

click to attach Web
page to e-mail
message

click to send text
content instead of
HTML code

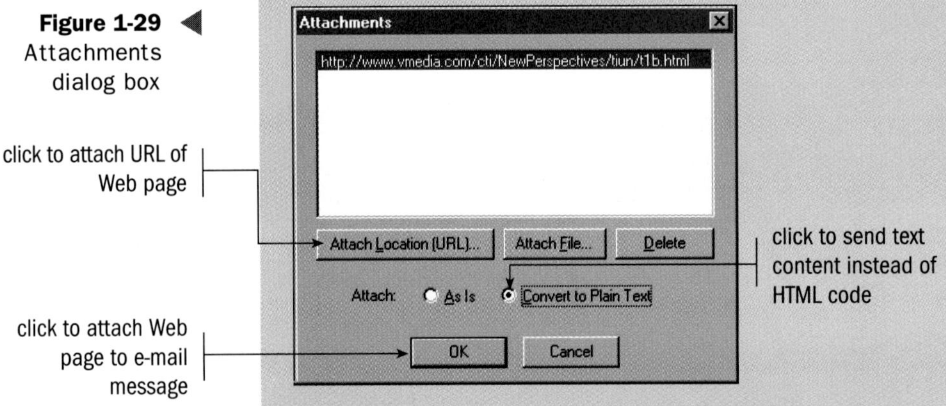

6. Click the **OK** button in the Attachments dialog box to close it and attach the entire current Web page to your e-mail message. The status message area of the dialog box reads "Loading attachment..."

7. Click the **Send** button 🖂 in the Mail window. Netscape dispatches your message and closes the dialog box.

   TROUBLE? If a message dialog box opens stating that "A network error occurred: unable to connect to server," then Netscape doesn't know where to send your e-mail. Click Options, click Mail and News Preferences, click the Servers tab, type the server name provided by your technical support person in the Outgoing Mail Server (SMTP) text box, click the OK button, and then click the Send button. The next time you check your e-mail, you'll have a message from yourself to which the text content of the Web page is attached.

Charlotte DuMont, another instructor at the workshop, has been taking notes about how to use Netscape, but wants to know what to do if she needs help and no one familiar with Netscape is around.

Getting Online Help

One of the best sources of information and help is always available when you're using Netscape. The **Netscape Handbook** is an online reference created and maintained by Netscape for use with its software; you can open the Handbook with either a toolbar button or from the Help menu. The Handbook provides tutorials that walk you through common procedures that you need to know in order to use Netscape. It also provides a reference section that you can access through the index. The entries are cross-referenced so that you can find a specific entry by looking it up under several topics. For example, the Viewing inline images entry is listed under I in the Images topics, under A in the Auto Load Images topics, and under L in the Load Images topics.

Even though the workshop members just saw how to load images automatically, Charlotte isn't sure she remembers the precise steps. She asks you to help her find information about setting the Auto Load Images option.

To get online Help:

1. Click the **Handbook** directory button to open Netscape's Online Handbook page. See Figure 1-30.

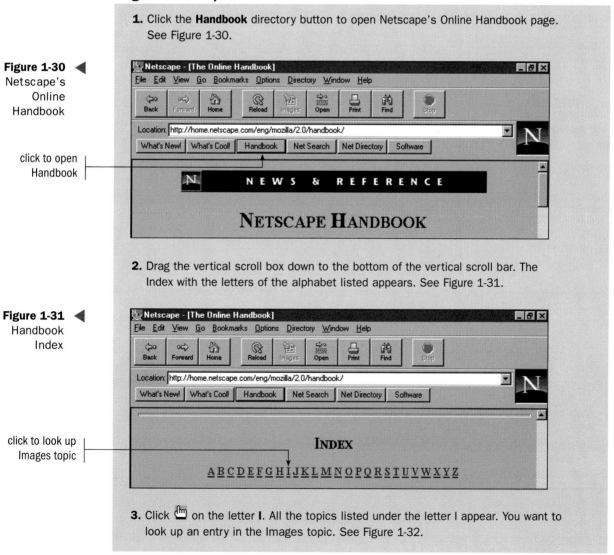

Figure 1-30
Netscape's
Online
Handbook

click to open
Handbook

2. Drag the vertical scroll box down to the bottom of the vertical scroll bar. The Index with the letters of the alphabet listed appears. See Figure 1-31.

Figure 1-31
Handbook
Index

click to look up
Images topic

3. Click 🖑 on the letter **I**. All the topics listed under the letter I appear. You want to look up an entry in the Images topic. See Figure 1-32.

Figure 1-32 ◀
Letter I topics

click this entry ————→

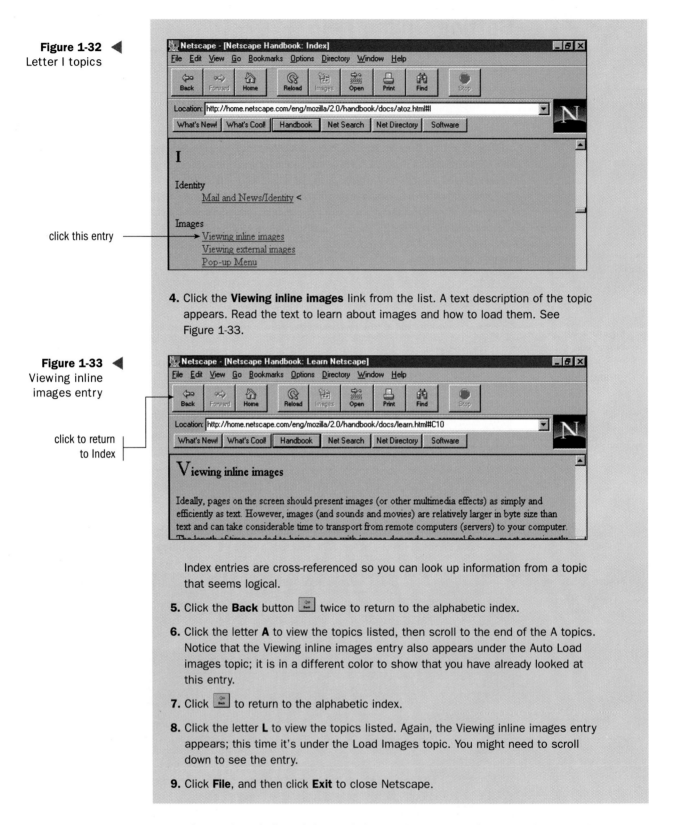

4. Click the **Viewing inline images** link from the list. A text description of the topic appears. Read the text to learn about images and how to load them. See Figure 1-33.

Figure 1-33 ◀
Viewing inline images entry

click to return to Index

Index entries are cross-referenced so you can look up information from a topic that seems logical.

5. Click the **Back** button ⬚ twice to return to the alphabetic index.

6. Click the letter **A** to view the topics listed, then scroll to the end of the A topics. Notice that the Viewing inline images entry also appears under the Auto Load images topic; it is in a different color to show that you have already looked at this entry.

7. Click ⬚ to return to the alphabetic index.

8. Click the letter **L** to view the topics listed. Again, the Viewing inline images entry appears; this time it's under the Load Images topic. You might need to scroll down to see the entry.

9. Click **File**, and then click **Exit** to close Netscape.

Stephan and Michelle end the workshop with comments from the educators about incorporating the Internet in their classes. Lyle mentions that the information superhighway might bridge some of the gaps between metropolitan and rural schools as well as between wealthy and disadvantaged districts by providing common, equally accessible, resources to all. As technology costs decrease and states encourage network connections in their public schools, distinctions such as these will begin to fade.

The teachers thank Michelle and Stephan for running such a helpful workshop. Michelle and Stephan, in turn, thank you for all your work. The workshop was such a success that they start planning another one.

Quick Check

1. True or False: The full filename in a URL must be unique within its own server but can be duplicated at other servers.

2. Three examples of URL protocol identifiers are _____, _____, and _____.

3. Is the Web page located at the URL http://www.CTI.COM/HOME.html the same as the Web page located at URL http://www.cti.com/home.html? Why or why not?

4. List two reasons you might receive an error message that states the URL location does not exist.

5. You can easily flip through Web pages using the _____, _____, and _____ toolbar buttons.

6. The Auto Load Images option lets you decide between _____ and _____.

7. True or False: A printed Web page cannot contain any graphics or special formatting.

8. When you append a Web page to your e-mail message, it is called an _____.

9. _____ is available in the Netscape Handbook.

Tutorial Assignments

Michelle and Stephan want to gear their next workshop for college-level educators. For their first workshop, they found a lot of material geared toward kindergarten through high school students. They need to find out how much the Internet is being used for educational purposes in higher education, what type of sites and information are available, and who is involved with this new approach to education.

They ask you to look at trends in the Internet and answer the following questions: How is the Internet affecting higher education? Do you think the trends overall will be positive? What are some of the possible negative side-effects?

Michelle suggested a few Web pages from which you can begin looking for answers. Do the following:

1. If necessary, launch Netscape.
2. Open the Web page at the URL "http://www.vmedia.com/cti/NewPerspectives/tiun."
3. Click the Tutorial Assignments and Case Problems link.
4. Scroll down until you see the Tutorial 1 Tutorial Assignments section.
5. Connect to the World Lecture Hall link in the "Universities Around the World" section.

6. Scan the page and see if you can find any information you can use to answer Stephan's and Michelle's questions.
7. Print Preview the World Lecture Hall page to find out how long it is.
8. Print the entire contents of the World Lecture Hall page from Print Preview, and then close Print Preview.
9. Return to the Tutorial Assignments and Case Problems page.
10. Connect to the Distance Education on the WWW link in the Tutorial 1 Tutorial Assignments section.

11. Scroll through the page. What are four main kinds of services? What is the relevance of the WWW to distance education?
12. Find out how many pages this Web page has. If it is more than two pages, do not print it.
13. Open the Mail Window to e-mail the Web page.

14. In the Mail To text box, type your intructor's e-mail address.
15. Attach the Distance Education on the WWW page to your e-mail.
16. Type your answers to the questions for Assignment 11 in the message box.
17. Send the e-mail.

Case Problems

1. University Informational Pages Karla Marletti, director of admissions at Southern University, noticed that an increasing number of universities are placing Web pages on the Internet. She wants her university to remain current in its use of technology and decides that the school should put a Web page on the WWW. She is not sure what layout or design would be most appealing for the page or what type of information should be included. She asks you to find a couple of Web pages that you think have attractive and effective designs with interesting and helpful content.

If necessary, start Netscape, and then do the following:

1. Open the Web page at the URL "http://www.vmedia.com/cti/NewPerspectives/tiun."
2. Click the Tutorial Assignments and Case Problems link.
3. Scroll down until you see the Tutorial 1 Case Problems section.
4. Connect to the University Information Pages link to find a listing of universities with Web pages.
5. Visit three Web pages for universities within the United States and then visit two Web pages for universities outside the United States.
6. Choose Web pages for two universities that you think have an unusual or attractive layout and interesting and relevant content.
7. Print Preview both Web pages and find out on how many pages they will print.
8. Print the shorter university Web page. On the hardcopy, explain what you liked about that Web page.
9. Attach the longer university Web page to an e-mail.
10. In the message box, explain what you liked about that Web page and make sure you include its URL.
11. Send the e-mail to your instructor.

2. The Fresno Daily Helen Wu is a staff journalist who specializes in researching and writing articles about trends in society for *The Fresno Daily*, a newspaper serving the Fresno, California community. She just received an assignment to write a feature article on how the Internet is changing the way people spend their leisure time. As part of her article, Helen wants to discuss the current size of the Internet and its rate of growth. She asks you to find statistics on the current number of Internet domains, the current number of Internet hosts, the current number of Web sites, and the percentage these figures have grown since they were counted last.

If necessary, launch Netscape, and then do the following:

1. Open the Web page at the URL "http://www.vmedia.com/cti/NewPerspectives/tiun."
2. Click the Tutorial Assignments and Case Problems link.
3. Scroll down until you see the Tutorial 1 Case Problems section.
4. Connect to The Fresno Daily link to find a listing of relevant Web pages.
5. Navigate through the Web pages to look for the statistics Helen needs.

6. When you find a Web page that contains a relevant statistic, look at that Web page in Print Preview.
7. Print only the page or pages that contain the information you need and then close Print Preview.

8. When you have all the information, write a short report about your findings in the message box of an e-mail.

9. Include the URL of each page you used in the text of your message. *Hint*: Check the header of the printed Web page.

10. Send the e-mail to your instructor.

3. The Carpet Shoppe The Carpet Shoppe imports and sells hand-woven rugs from Thailand, Burma, and India. Established in 1987, the shop has become very successful. Four times each year, Al Sanchez, the owner, travels to these countries to replenish his inventory of new carpets.

Although the shop has operated efficiently without a computer, Al has decided that it's time to convert to computerized inventory and accounting systems. Al isn't sure whether to purchase a Macintosh or an IBM-compatible system. He wants a portable computer that he could bring on his buying trips. With a laptop computer, not only will he have the most current figures at his fingertips, but he also will be able to communicate with his employees at home without worrying about the time difference or the cost of international phone calls. He wants a top-of-the-line notebook computer that won't become obsolete quickly. The more RAM, the bigger the disk storage space, and the faster the modem, the better.

He asks you to find information such as the model name, model number, and features about different brands of computers. Most of the bigger computer manufacturers place Web pages on the Internet with their latest computer models and prices, so you can begin looking there.

If necessary, launch Netscape, and then do the following:

1. Open the Web page at the URL "http://www.vmedia.com/cti/NewPerspectives/tiun."

2. Click the Tutorial Assignments and Case Problems link.

3. Scroll down until you see the Tutorial 1 Case Problems section.

4. Click the Carpet Shoppe link to find a listing of relevant Web pages.

5. Find information about a top-of-the line notebook computer from Apple.

6. Print Preview any Web pages that contain information Al wants to see.

7. Print only those pages that contain relevant information.

8. Find information about a top-of-the line notebook computer from IBM.

9. Print Preview any Web pages that contain information Al wants to see.

10. Print only those pages that contain relevant information.

11. Write a summary report of the information you found, and make a recommendation of which notebook computer you think Al should buy.

4. Marketing 305 Consumer Behavior The students of Marketing 305 (MK305) have prepared a survey to study consumer behavior in online environments. They want to determine people's perceptions about shopping on the Internet. They plan to compile a report that discusses what consumer's think about two malls available on the Internet, how products prices compare to their local malls, and what percentage of people are willing to shop online.

If necessary, launch Netscape, and then do the following:

1. Open the Web page at the URL "http://www.vmedia.com/cti/NewPerspectives/tiun."

2. Click the Tutorial Assignments and Case Problems link.

3. Scroll down until you see the Tutorial 1 Case Problems section.

4. Click the MK305 Survey link to find a listing of online shopping mall Web pages.

5. Navigate through two online shopping malls looking at various products.

6. Print out one sample product description from each mall. Preview each Web page to make sure it won't be longer than one page.

7. Compare a similar product available at each mall. Look how information about the product is presented as well as its price.
8. Return to the Tutorial Assignments and Case Problems page and locate the MK305 survey link.
9. Connect to the MK305 survey page.
10. Answer the survey questions. When you are done, click the Submit button.
11. E-mail the completed survey to your instructor.

Lab Assignments

This Lab Assignment is designed to accompany the interactive Course Lab called Internet World Wide Web. **To start the Lab using Windows 95**, click the Start button on the Windows 95 taskbar, point to Programs, point to Course Labs, point to New Perspectives Applications, and click Internet World Wide Web. **To start the Lab using Windows 3.1**, double-click the Course Labs for the Internet group icon to open a window containing the Lab icons, then double-click the Internet World Wide Web icon. If you do not see Course Labs on your Windows 95 Program menu, or if you do not see the Course Labs for the Internet group icon in your Windows 3.1 Program Manager window, see your instructor or technical support person.

The Internet World Wide Web One of the most popular services on the Internet is the World Wide Web. This Lab is a Web simulator that teaches you how to use Web browser software to find information. You can use this Lab whether or not your school provides you with Internet access.

1. Click the Steps button to learn how to use Web browser software. As you proceed through the Steps, answer all of the Quick Check questions that appear. After you complete the Steps, you will see a Quick Check Summary Report. Follow the instructions on the screen to print this report.
2. Click the Explore button on the Welcome screen. Use the Web browser to locate a weather map of the Carribean Virgin Islands. What is its URL?
3. Enter the URL **http://www.atour.com**. A SCUBA diver named Wadson Lachouffe has been searching for the fabled treasure of Greybeard the pirate. A link from the Adventure Travel Web site leads to a Wadson's Web page called "Hidden Treasure." Locate the Hidden Treasure page and answer the following questions:
   a. What was the name of Greybeard's ship?
   b. What was Greybeard's favorite food?
   c. What does Wadson think happened to Greybeard's ship?
4. In the Steps, you found a graphic of Jupiter from the photo archives of the Jet Propulsion Laboratory. In the Explore section of the Lab, you can also find a graphic of Saturn. Suppose one of your friends wanted a picture of Saturn for an astronomy report. Make a list of the blue, underlined links your friend must click to find the Saturn graphic. Assume that your friend will begin at the Web Trainer home page.
5. Jump back to the Adventure Travel Web site. Write a one-page description of the information at the site, the number of pages the site contains, and a diagram of the links it contains.
6. Chris Thomson, a student at UVI, has his own Web page. In Explore, look at the information Chris has included on his pages. Suppose you could create your own Web page. What would you include? Use word processing software to design your own Web page. Make sure you indicate the graphics and links you would use.

Finding What's Out There

Using the Internet as a Resource at the
Peter H. Martin Public Library

Peter H. Martin Public Library

CASE

The Peter H. Martin Library is a well-established public library supported by local and federal government funding as well as local civic groups. Last year, the Board of Directors, which decides the library's policies and spending, faced several challenges. The money available for the budget was shrinking; costs to purchase new books, supplies, and other holdings were increasing; the building was nearing its capacity; and the community wanted the library open longer hours and an outreach program set up to provide service to homebound citizens. About the same time, a state conference offered a session on Internet use by government institutions. Several Board members who attended the session decided that the Internet could help solve some of the library's problems. The Board authorized Anna Ferri, the library's technical assistant, to develop and implement a plan that incorporates Internet access to expand the library's existing resources.

Anna inventoried the available library resources. She found that the library already had an Internet connection to a host computer within the city and a **local area network** (LAN), a group of computers in one location that are connected so they can share data, files, and software. The library's LAN connects the microcomputers throughout the building to the **server** (a computer that stores the data and programs accessed by other computers in the LAN) in Anna's office. One of the programs on the LAN is a computerized cataloging system that it shares via the Internet with other regional libraries. Visitors can search for books at any participating library by title, author, or subject.

The Board doesn't want the community to think that the current library is obsolete. Instead, Anna must convey that any changes she makes, such as providing additional online services, supplement, rather than replace, the library's holdings. To fulfill these goals, Anna:

- Created a home page that gives information about the library's services and layout.

- Installed Netscape on the server so all the library's computers have Internet access.

- Added technical support for library users who dial into the system from their home computers.

- Organized training sessions for library personnel and the general public on how to use the Internet as a research and reference tool.

The response from the community so far has been very positive. Because of the library's Internet access, more people are spending time there researching topics for business, school, and personal enjoyment. The library staff spends a lot of time showing people how to surf the Internet and find information. **Surfing** implies that you browse or skim all available information rather than read detailed information about a single topic. Anna asks you to work at the Help Desk, assisting the library staff in answering questions about the Internet.

SESSION

2.1

In this session, you will listen to an audio clip; use popular navigational guides; browse sites; view the history log; and add, use, and delete bookmarks.

Listening to an Audio Clip

Two teenagers, Sasha and Janine, stop by the Help Desk and ask you about the library's new Internet connection. You suggest that they begin by looking at the library's home page. Anna created the home page to orient visitors to the library's setup, tell them about the available services, and personally welcome them to the library with an audio clip.

To open the Peter H. Martin Library home page and listen to an audio clip:

1. Launch Netscape and make sure the Show Toolbar, Show Location, Show Directory Buttons, and Auto Load Images options are toggled on.

2. Click the **Open** button ⬛. The Open Location dialog box opens.

3. Type **http://www.vmedia.com/cti/NewPerspectives/tiun** in the Open Location text box, and then click the **Open** button to connect to the New Perspectives on the Internet Using Netscape Navigator page.

   TROUBLE? If a message dialog box opens stating that Netscape is unable to locate the server, you might have typed the URL incorrectly. Click the OK button to close the dialog box. If the URL in the location box does not match the one in Step 3, double-click in the location box, use the arrow keys to move the insertion point to any error, correct it, and then press the Enter key. If the URL is correct, press the Enter key to try again.

4. Click the **Tutorial 2** link to open the library's home page.

Figure 2-1 ◄
Peter H. Martin
Library home
page

click to hear
audio clip

position pointer here

audio filename

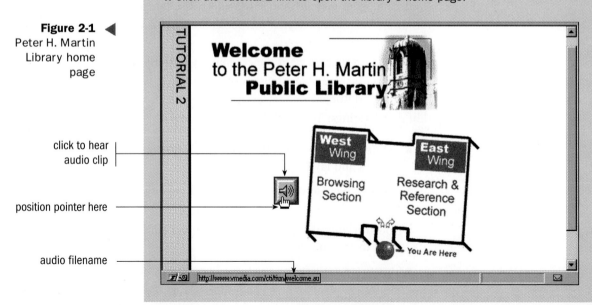

5. Position your pointer over the Audio button ⏸ on the Peter H. Martin Library home page. The URL in the status message area has the filename extension .AU, indicating the file type. See Figure 2-1. Whenever you see a filename extension that indicates an audio clip, Netscape might display a message dialog box asking you to indicate how it should handle the file.

6. Click ⏸ to open a playback device, similar to the one shown in Figure 2-2. A Viewing Location dialog box might open as the audio clip loads.

Figure 2-2 ◀
Playback
device

click to play
audio clip

Some sound drivers automatically play the audio file after the file loads, whereas others require you to press the Play button.

7. If the status message area indicates that the file is loaded, but you don't hear anything, click the **Play** button to hear the audio clip.

TROUBLE? If you do not hear any sound after clicking the Play button on the playback device, your computer might not have audio capabilities or the sound is turned down. Check with your instructor or technical support person.

TROUBLE? If the Unknown File Type dialog box opens, your Netscape installation does not recognize this type of audio file and you cannot hear the audio clip. Click the Cancel button to close the dialog box and continue with the tutorial.

8. Click the Close button ☒ in the upper-right corner of the playback device to close it, if necessary.

Sound, added to text and images, helps to make a Web page much more dynamic and "alive" than a static printed page. Being able to hear someone greet you to a page is much more welcoming than reading those same words. With sounds on a Web page, you can hear the roar of a lion, listen to the beat of a healthy heart, and play the latest song from your favorite band.

Any sound on a Web page is actually a file, which can be stored in different formats. Some formats provide a better-quality sound, but create a large audio file. Other formats optimize space, creating smaller audio files, but provide a lesser-quality sound. Audio is generally stored in two ways. The first is a digital representation, like a CD recording, and is often designated with the filename extensions .AU or. WAV. The second way instructs your computer how to simulate the sounds, like the notes on sheet music, and is often designated by the filename extension .MID. With another audio file format, Real Audio (.RAM), your computer plays the beginning of the audio clip while the later sections transfer to your machine, shortening the time you wait before hearing sound.

Each type of audio file needs to be interpreted by a **playback device**, software that understands a specific audio file extension. Not all software works with every type of audio file. When you link to an audio file, Netscape determines whether it will be able to interpret and play the sound using a program that comes with the Netscape software or one that you have installed on your computer. Netscape's built-in helper software can read some file types, such as .AU.

If the audio file being transferred cannot be interpreted by an existing program on Netscape's **Helper list** (a list of separate software to read audio, video, and image files stored on your computer), Netscape opens the Unknown File Type dialog box from which you can:

- Save the file to a disk and find a computer on which you can listen to it.
- Cancel the transfer.
- Select another program, which can interpret the sound file, to launch and add it to Netscape's Helper list.

Although the program needed to play a certain audio file might be on your computer or your LAN, you might need to add it to Netscape's Helper list, which is stored on the Options menu. Also, because new methods for encoding audio appear frequently, you might need to load additional software onto your computer to read the new type of file. Whenever you install new helper software on your computer or network, you need to update Netscape's Helper list.

Sasha and Janine want to know how to surf the Internet. Because they don't want to visit a particular site or locate any special information, you decide to introduce them to Netscape's What's Cool and What's New sites.

Surfing with Netscape's Guides

Just as you might flip through magazines or browse through books in a bookstore, sometimes you might want to randomly link from Web site to Web site, looking at pictures and reading fragments of text. To do this, you need a Web page, or link, as a starting point. Netscape has two sites that are good places to start surfing—the What's Cool site and the What's New site. These sites act as guides for you. You can get to either site from any Web page by using the directory buttons or the menu bar.

USES AND **abuses**

SURFING THE NET

People browse from site to site on the Web for many reasons. Some of the most common reasons you might surf are to:

- Expand your knowledge on nearly any topic.
- Find out about current events from around the world on electronic newspapers.
- Discover the culture and geography of other nations.
- Learn about tourism for particular countries, cities, and states.
- Read entertainment reviews and excerpts.

Finding What's Cool

With so much information available on the WWW, many people spend their time searching for unique and interesting sites, which often have unusual layouts or include interesting text, graphics, or sounds. Some individuals and organizations try to sell products or services whereas others want only to entertain or inform. Netscape Communications Corporation routinely scouts the Internet for unusual sites and then places links to those URLs on its What's Cool page. Netscape updates the list periodically, so it's a good starting point for surfing. You can find similar types of lists on the WWW compiled by other groups or individuals.

Sasha wants to check out the links on the What's Cool page first.

To look at the What's Cool list:

1. Click the **What's Cool** directory button to link to a list of unusual Web pages collected by Netscape Communications Corporation. See Figure 2-3. Netscape frequently updates the list and images to keep the content "cool."

Figure 2-3
What's Cool
Web page

click to open
Netscape's list of
"cool" sites

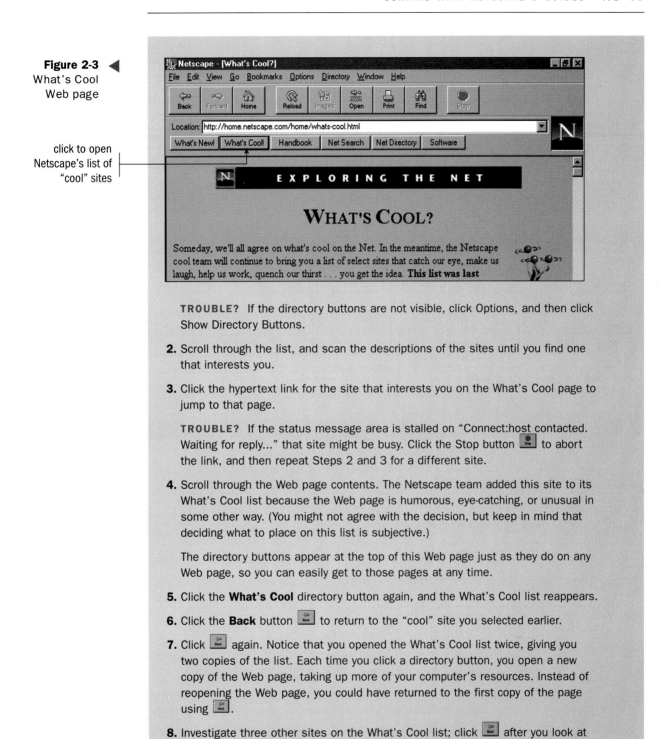

TROUBLE? If the directory buttons are not visible, click Options, and then click Show Directory Buttons.

2. Scroll through the list, and scan the descriptions of the sites until you find one that interests you.

3. Click the hypertext link for the site that interests you on the What's Cool page to jump to that page.

   TROUBLE? If the status message area is stalled on "Connect:host contacted. Waiting for reply..." that site might be busy. Click the Stop button to abort the link, and then repeat Steps 2 and 3 for a different site.

4. Scroll through the Web page contents. The Netscape team added this site to its What's Cool list because the Web page is humorous, eye-catching, or unusual in some other way. (You might not agree with the decision, but keep in mind that deciding what to place on this list is subjective.)

   The directory buttons appear at the top of this Web page just as they do on any Web page, so you can easily get to those pages at any time.

5. Click the **What's Cool** directory button again, and the What's Cool list reappears.

6. Click the **Back** button to return to the "cool" site you selected earlier.

7. Click again. Notice that you opened the What's Cool list twice, giving you two copies of the list. Each time you click a directory button, you open a new copy of the Web page, taking up more of your computer's resources. Instead of reopening the Web page, you could have returned to the first copy of the page using.

8. Investigate three other sites on the What's Cool list; click after you look at each site to return to the What's Cool list instead of using the directory button to open additional copies of the What's Cool page.

Now that Sasha and Janine have looked at some unusual sites on the What's Cool page, Janine wants to know how the list on Netscape's What's New page is different.

Finding What's New

The amount of information on the WWW is immense and growing daily. It is difficult, if not impossible, to find and visit all the new sites added daily. Instead, Netscape's team compiles a list of new Web pages at its What's New site. Anyone can submit the name and URL of a new page for the What's New list, but Netscape reserves the right to accept or reject any entry. In general, Netscape lists sites that also apply some new technique or technology. Other organizations that maintain similar types of lists might have different rules and regulations about how they collect and qualify new sites.

Janine and Sasha want to see the sites Netscape has compiled on its What's New list.

To look at the What's New list:

1. Click the **What's New** directory button to connect to a list of new Web sites compiled by Netscape. See Figure 2-4. Netscape frequently updates the list and images to keep the content "new."

Figure 2-4 ◀
What's New
Web page

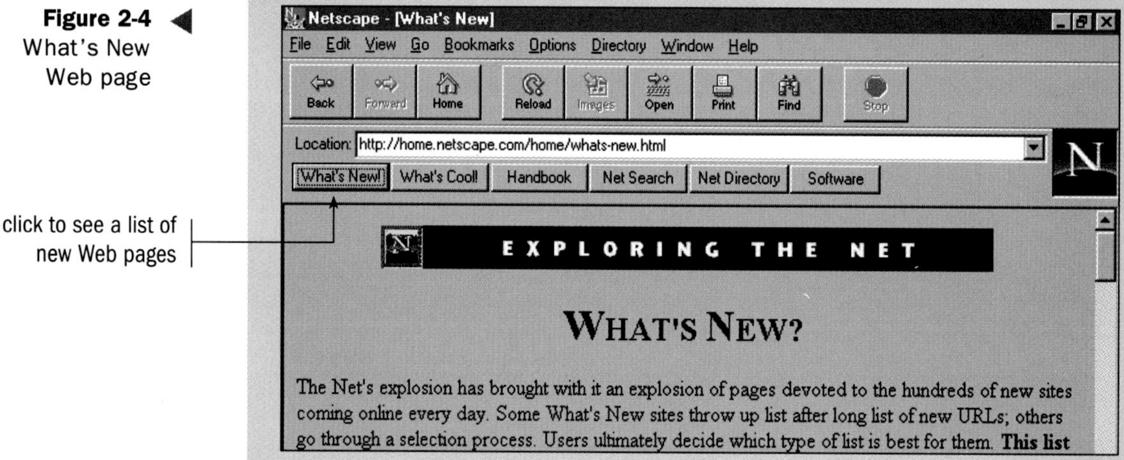

click to see a list of
new Web pages

2. Scroll through the list and scan the descriptions of the sites until you find one that interests you.

3. Click the hypertext link on the What's New page for a site that interests you to jump to that page.

   TROUBLE? If the status message area is stalled on, "Connect:host contacted. Waiting for reply..." that site might be busy. Click the Stop button 🔲 to abort the link, and then repeat Steps 2 and 3 for another site.

4. Scroll through the page contents. The Netscape team added this site to its What's New list because the content or design of this Web page contains references to new technology. (You might not agree with the decision, but like the What's Cool list, deciding what to place on this list is subjective.)

5. Click the **Back** button 🔲 to return to the What's New list.

6. Investigate three other sites; click 🔲 after you look at each site to return to the What's New list instead of opening additional copies of the page.

One disadvantage to sites on both the What's New and What's Cool lists is that the lists are frequented by many people and the pages suddenly can become extremely popular. These pages are usually maintained by modest-sized servers, incapable of handling the large volume of requests. As a result, you'll often be unable to link to these pages or even to different pages housed on the same server. Figure 2-5 illustrates this problem.

Figure 2-5 ◀
Popular Web
page blocks
access to other
Web pages on
same server

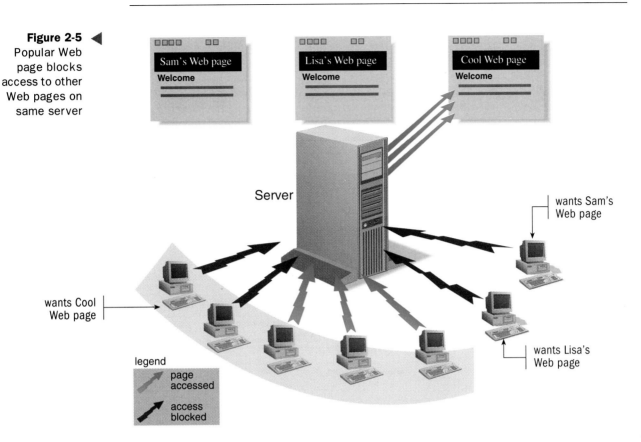

To avoid the congestion of trying to access pages from these two popular lists, you decide to show Sasha and Janine some other guides that Anna included on the library's Web page.

Using a Navigational Guide

Many individuals and organizations provide navigational guide services similar to Netscape's What's Cool and What's New pages. A **navigational guide** compiles a list or index of Web pages organized around a general theme or subject. Each list has its own style, formatting, and frequency of updates.

Anna designed the Browsing Section page to match the look and organization of the browsing section in the library. The floor plan is reproduced on the page so that people familiar with the library's setup who are using the library's pages from home will know where to go to find information. Also, Anna thought the floor plan would help home-bound users feel more connected to the library building. She regularly updates the list of navigational guides to ensure that the links are current and available.

You'll show Janine and Sasha the Browsing Section page now.

To enter the library's Browsing Section:

1. Click the **Back** button 🔲 on the toolbar until you return to the Peter H. Martin Library home page.

   TROUBLE? If you can't find the library home page, repeat Steps 1 through 4 in the earlier section "Listening to an Audio Clip."

2. Place the pointer over **Browsing Section** on the left side of the floor plan. See Figure 2-6.

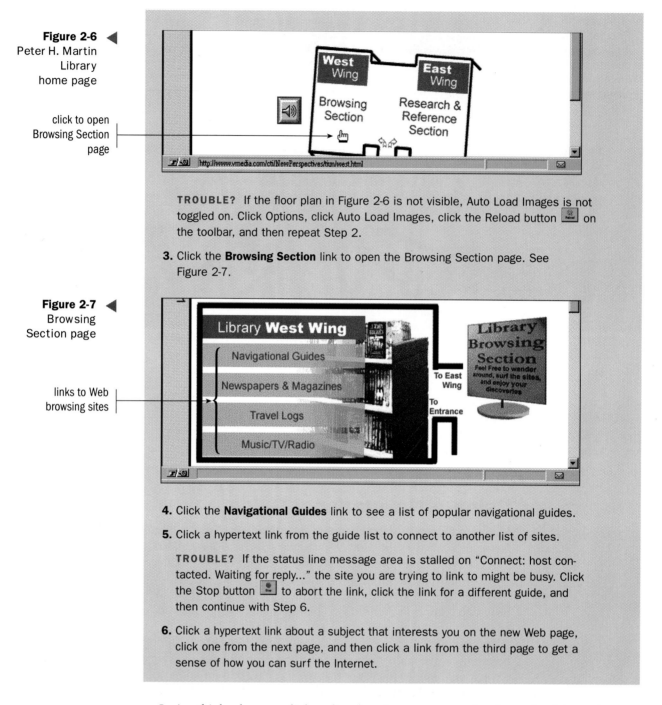

Figure 2-6
Peter H. Martin
Library
home page

click to open
Browsing Section
page

TROUBLE? If the floor plan in Figure 2-6 is not visible, Auto Load Images is not toggled on. Click Options, click Auto Load Images, click the Reload button [image] on the toolbar, and then repeat Step 2.

3. Click the **Browsing Section** link to open the Browsing Section page. See Figure 2-7.

Figure 2-7
Browsing
Section page

links to Web
browsing sites

4. Click the **Navigational Guides** link to see a list of popular navigational guides.

5. Click a hypertext link from the guide list to connect to another list of sites.

TROUBLE? If the status line message area is stalled on "Connect: host contacted. Waiting for reply..." the site you are trying to link to might be busy. Click the Stop button [image] to abort the link, click the link for a different guide, and then continue with Step 6.

6. Click a hypertext link about a subject that interests you on the new Web page, click one from the next page, and then click a link from the third page to get a sense of how you can surf the Internet.

Janine thinks she saw a link earlier that she wants to try, but it was back several pages. Sasha wants to know if he can view the series of links they just followed.

Using the History Log

Netscape tracks the URL of every Web page you visit on the Go menu. The **history log** is a list of sites that you have visited since launching Netscape. From the history log, you can see the path you took to get to the latest page or skip directly to a site you visited earlier. The top entry in the history log, numbered "0," is your most recent URL connection. The bottom entry is the home page you saw when you started Netscape. A check mark indicates your current location. As long as you continue to connect to sites, additional entries appear at the top of the list.

You can repeatedly click the Back button to return to any site you already visited, but choosing a site from the history log is usually quicker and easier. If you click the Back button until you return to your home page and then click on a link, Netscape clears the current history log and begins a new one.

To use the history log:

1. Click **Go** to open the Go menu and see the history log. See Figure 2-8. The history log on your menu will be different from the one shown in Figure 2-8 because you linked to sites based on your own interests.

Figure 2-8 ◀
Go menu

current Web page —

visited sites —

click to return to
Browsing section

home page —

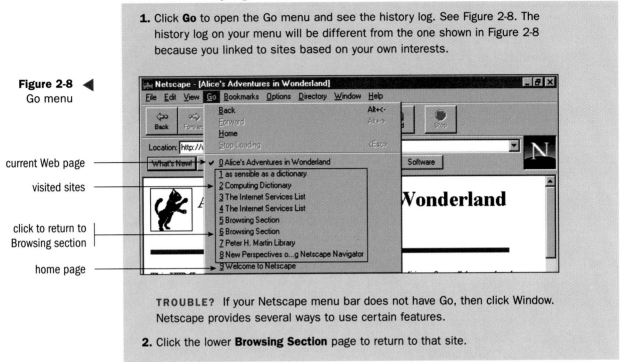

TROUBLE? If your Netscape menu bar does not have Go, then click Window. Netscape provides several ways to use certain features.

2. Click the lower **Browsing Section** page to return to that site.

You leave Sasha and Janine surfing the Net to help the Runyan family, who are planning their next vacation. They want to use the Internet to investigate travel destinations. Because they don't have a specific place in mind, you decide to show them the library's travel guide site.

To access the Peter H. Martin Library travel sources:

1. Click the **Travel Logs** link on the Browsing Section page to open a list of travel links. See Figure 2-9.

Figure 2-9 ◀
Travel sites

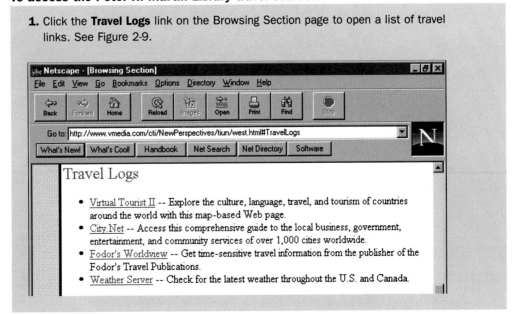

2. Click the **Virtual Tourist II** link then scroll down to see a map of the world. See Figure 2-10.

Figure 2-10 ◀
Virtual Tourist
II Web page

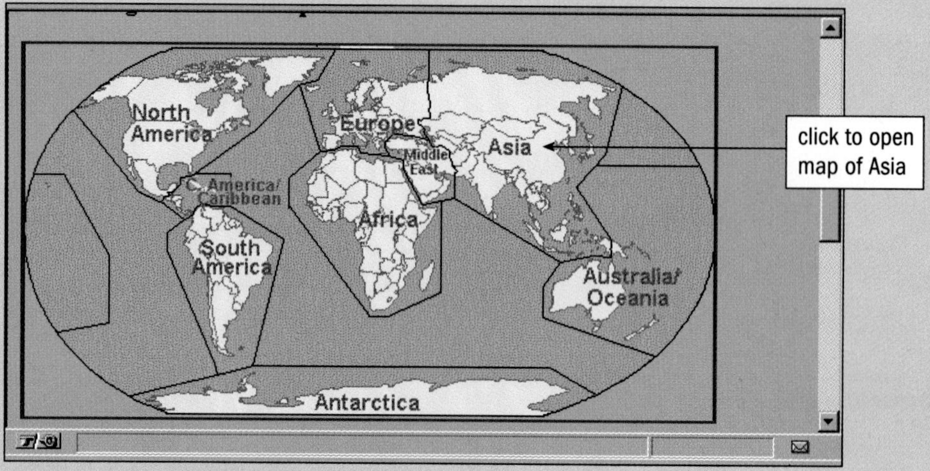

click to open
map of Asia

TROUBLE? If the Virtual Tourist II site is busy, try another travel link. It might not be map-oriented but will still contain links to travel destinations.

The Virtual Tourist II page is a visual presentation of links rather than text. You can click any point on the map to link to a different page and get additional information about that country or region.

3. Click **Asia** to open a map of Asia.

4. Click **India** to link to its travel page. See Figure 2-11.

Figure 2-11 ◀
Travel links

additional links

India

Cities
Bangalore
Bombay
Calcutta
Chandigarh
Hyderabad
Kozhikode
Madras

TROUBLE? If the India site is busy or you are on a travel Web page other than Virtual Tourist II, click another link until you find one that is available.

Conrad Runyan tells his wife and children that he's always wanted to visit India. He'd like to explore this page some more. However, his family wants to keep looking at other places. You'll show Conrad how to mark this Web page so he can easily find it later.

Using Bookmarks

While surfing the Net, you might find an interesting or unusual site to which you want to return. Rather than trying to remember the URL of that site, you can mark it with a **bookmark**, which is a shortcut back to a Web site. Just as you insert a piece of paper into a printed book to locate a specific page, you can add a bookmark to locate a specific Web page and, later, access or delete them.

Netscape typically stores bookmarks in a file named bookmark.htm on your computer's hard disk. In this case, the bookmarks reside only on the computer where you add them, not on another computer. If you add a bookmark for a Web page on your computer and want to show that page to someone else on another computer, you'll need to know its URL or how you can link to it. If you use a variety of computers and want to create a list of bookmarks that you can use on any machine with Netscape, just store the bookmark file on a disk.

You suggest to the Runyan family that they create a bookmark file on a disk so they can take it with them and use it when they access the Internet with Netscape from their home computer.

To create a bookmark file:

1. Click **Bookmarks** on the menu bar, and then click **Go to Bookmarks** to open the Netscape Bookmarks window, which contains a directory of all the bookmarks on that computer. See Figure 2-12. Remember that the list of bookmarks will be different for your computer.

Figure 2-12 ◀
Library's
bookmarks list

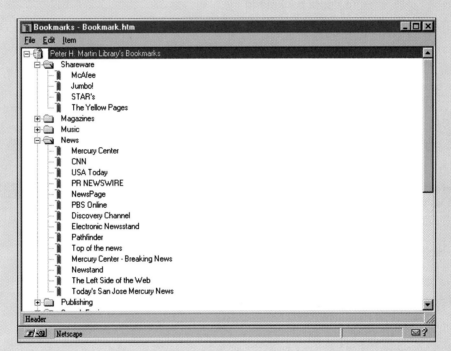

TROUBLE? If you don't see Go to Bookmarks, click Window, then click Bookmarks to open the bookmark file.

2. Insert your Student Disk into drive A or the appropriate drive on your computer.

3. Click **File**, and then click **Save As** on the Bookmarks menu bar to open the Save bookmarks file.

4. Type **a:\bookmark.htm** in the File name text box, and then press the Enter key. A copy of the bookmarks list saves to your disk. You can delete some of these bookmarks later, but for now you'll add to this file.

5. Click **File**, and then click **Open** on the Bookmarks menu bar. The Open bookmarks file dialog box opens.

6. Click **bookmark.htm** in the file list, and then press the Enter key to open the bookmark file on your disk. The Bookmarks window might show the bookmark file on your disk rather than the bookmark file on your computer. Any bookmarks you add to the file will affect only your copy.

7. Click **File**, and then click **Close** to exit the Bookmarks window.

With a disk all ready to save bookmarks to, Conrad wants to add a bookmark for the India page so he can look at it again from home.

Adding a Bookmark

A bookmark is helpful when you want to return to a specific Web site, try other links from that page, or show someone else a certain site. You can add a bookmark for any Web page by using the Bookmarks menu.

From their home computer, every member of the Runyan family plans to look for Web pages on places they would like to visit. Instead of having to write down a list of URLs, they can add a bookmark for any page a member of the family finds interesting. Then the rest of the family can look at these pages when they have time. You'll show Conrad and his family how to place a bookmark for the India page on the disk file they created. When the family leaves, they can take the bookmark file with them.

To add a bookmark:

1. Click **Bookmarks** to open the Bookmarks menu. Remember that the list of bookmarks is unique for every computer. If you select any bookmark that ends with a triangle, or **header**, an additional list of bookmarks opens.

2. Click **Add Bookmark** to add a shortcut to the current Web page.

3. Click **Bookmarks** again to open the menu and display the list of bookmarks including one for the India Web page, which is probably at the end of the list. Notice that the page is listed by its title, which is more descriptive than its URL. See Figure 2-13.

Figure 2-13 ◄
Updated
Bookmarks
menu

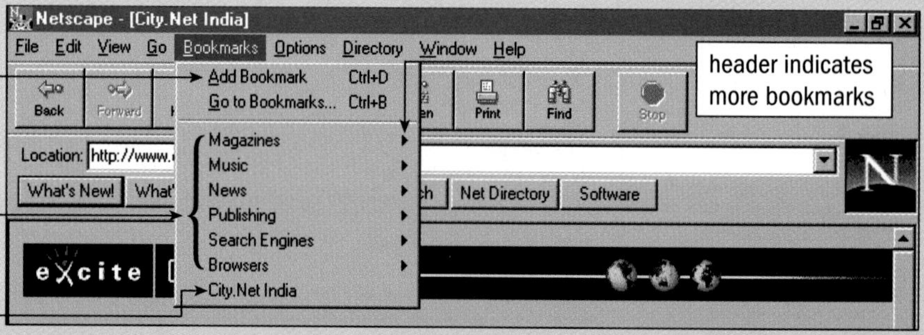

click to add
bookmark for current
Web page

your list will differ

new bookmark

header indicates
more bookmarks

TROUBLE? If the India Web page bookmark is not on your bookmarks list, you might have added a bookmark for a different Web page. Check the title of the current Web page, and then look for a bookmark that matches it. If you still don't see the bookmark, click any bookmark titles with a header to see additional bookmarks. If you still can't find the bookmark, repeat Steps 1 and 2.

4. Click **Bookmarks** again to close the menu, then click the **Back** button [ ] twice to move to a different Web page.

Now that the Web page for which you added a bookmark is no longer the current page, you can show the Runyan family how to refer back to it.

Accessing a Bookmark

Because the menu bar is available no matter what Web page you are looking at or how long you have been surfing, you can click a bookmark to directly return to that Web page. A bookmark is available until you delete it from the list or the bookmark file is altered.

You'll show Conrad how to get back to the India Web page.

To access a bookmark:

1. Click **Bookmarks** to see the Web page bookmark you just added.

2. Click **City.Net India** or the bookmark you added to return to that Web page.

The Runyans are glad to see that bookmarks are so easy to use. Luisa Runyan wants to know how to remove a bookmark from the list if the URL of a Web page changes or the family no longer wants to look at a certain page.

Deleting a Bookmark

Deleting, or erasing, bookmarks is almost as easy as adding them. It's always a good idea to delete the bookmark for any Web page that you no longer use or that has become outdated. This will help keep your list of bookmarks manageable and organized.

Because the Runyans copied the list of bookmarks from the library's file, the family's file contains some unwanted bookmarks. You'll show them how to delete these extra bookmarks.

REFERENCE
window

DELETING A BOOKMARK

- Click Bookmarks, and then click Go to Bookmarks.
- Click the bookmark you want to delete.
- Click Edit, and then click Delete.
- Click File, and then click Close.

To delete a bookmark:

1. Click **Bookmarks**, and then click **Go to Bookmarks** to open the Netscape Bookmarks window, which contains a list of all the bookmarks in that file. Remember that your list of bookmarks will be different.

2. Click a bookmark from the list to highlight a bookmark you want to remove.

3. Click **Edit**, and then click **Delete** to remove the highlighted bookmark from the list.

4. Repeat Steps 2 and 3 to remove any other bookmarks you don't want from your file.

5. Click **File**, and then click **Close** to close the Netscape Bookmarks dialog box.

USES AND abuses

POTENTIAL REGULATION OF THE INTERNET

One of the Net's most powerful traits is its openness. Anyone can add files to or copy files from the Internet; no restrictions limit the content of these files. As a result, some government officials want to create laws that control the content and use of the Web.

- Many people feel that any government regulation will violate individual freedoms. The Internet spans nations, cultures, age groups, and legal systems, creating an entity that has no walls or borders. While one government might impose regulations, these laws do not apply to citizens of other nations. Nor can a government prohibit its citizens from visiting Internet sites in other nations. To do so destroys the very foundation of the Internet, according to opponents of regulation.

- Alternatives to regulation do exist. Each service provider could take responsibility for documents accessed through its server site and control the pages accessed there.

- For child protection, special programs exist that scan every file or Web document as it is retrieved by a computer for phrases that indicate inappropriate material. The monitoring program automatically closes a document when it finds a match. Many Internet users think that supervising what children can access, as is done with cable television, movies, and music, is more equitable than government regulation.

The Runyans thank you for your instruction and leave for home eager to explore further the travel information available on the Internet.

Quick Check

1. The term _____ means connecting from site to site using hypertext links to follow topics of interest.

2. True or False: Netscape uses its own software to interpret every type of file format.

3. To see a current list of unusual Web sites, you can go to Netscape's _____ page.

4. A disadvantage to using a URL link placed on the What's New page is a(n) _____ demand for the URL's server.

5. General purpose navigational guides to the WWW usually categorize, or index, links by _____.

6. After browsing a number of Internet sites, you can trace your path by viewing the _____ from the Go menu.

7. You can use a _____ to mark a Web page you might want to visit again.

8. True or False: Bookmarks are listed by only their URL in the bookmark list.

You have completed Session 2.1. If you aren't going to work through Session 2.2 now, you should exit Netscape. When you are ready to start Session 2.2, start Netscape, make sure the Show Toolbar, Show Location, Show Directory Buttons, and Auto Load Images options are toggled on, open the URL http://www.vmedia.com/cti/NewPerspectives/tiun and then click the Tutorial 2 link to return to the Peter H. Martin Library home page, then continue with the session.

In this session, you will conduct search queries by content and by subject, visit a converted Gopher site, use search engines and spiders, save documents and images to a file, and copy to the clipboard.

Searching by Content

Libraries manage reference sections holding volumes of microfiche and document collections and hire trained reference librarians. Many of the reference materials in question have been converted to CD-ROM and other disk file storage media that allow computer access. For years, the Internet provided academic researchers with links to some of these computer files. More recently, the debut of the World Wide Web (WWW) has prompted increased use of these materials and encouraged the creation of easier-to-use searching techniques. Many text-based files were converted to Web pages that offer custom charting or graphs based upon questions people ask. What's more, tapping into the Internet's resources provides access to documents, files, and computers worldwide.

As mentioned earlier, surfing is a slow-paced, read-for-pleasure type of activity. Another, more focused, use of the Internet involves fact gathering and research. You might use the Internet to find information about a term-paper topic, to learn about opening a new business, or to report statistics to a government agency. A common thread in all these research goals is that they have a specific topic, or theme.

Yoko Muramoto approaches you at the Help Desk to get assistance in finding information about opening a take-out restaurant serving Japanese food. She is in the early stages of planning and needs to answer many questions before deciding to proceed. Some questions include: What is the population of the area? What are the current interest rates for bank loans? What government resources exist for small businesses? The answers to these questions and many others can be found on the Internet, but locating the information might be challenging.

USES AND abuses

RESEARCHING

The Internet is a vast international research tool that people use to locate sources for personal, academic, professional, and business projects. The Web is fast becoming a popular spot to research information because you can:

- Access references around the world immediately.
- Read the latest information posted about a topic.
- Find related topics easily with hypertext links.
- Sift through thousands of documents quickly with keyword queries.
- Supplement traditional library references with Internet sources.

To manage the growing number of files and documents, Internet servers and commercial organizations collect information and store it in databases. A **database** is a collection of related information that can be searched by topic. The database software contains a **search engine**, which retrieves information from the database based upon a person's query. A **query** is a written request in question form that tells the search engine to find documents that contain a **keyword** (a specified word or phrase). For example, Yoko might want to search for information that matches the keywords "population statistics." The search engine generates a list of sites on the Internet that contain those words.

Writing Search Queries

Every search query you write must be in the proper query language so that the search engine you are using can interpret the request. A **query language** is a set of rules, or **syntax**, that you must follow when forming a query. A query can consist of one or more keywords and a default comparison operator, such as "and," which you don't need to type in the query. A search engine that uses a simple query language checks for a match on a specific word. Either the word is found or it is not. A search engine that uses a more sophisticated language can search for multiple words, and you can choose whether one or all the words must be found if the document is to be considered a match. For example, the list resulting from the query "university" and "college" would include any document that contains some mention of both words. The query "university" or "college," produces a much larger list because any document with either word would be included. Finally, a search engine that uses a highly sophisticated query language can search for the specific words in the query and make assumptions about the appropriateness of that information based on the words' use and context.

Each query language sets a standard operator as a default, which you do not need to type in the query. For example, some query languages assume "or" as the comparison operator whereas others assume "and." Before you use a new search engine, you'll need to determine what query language it uses and how you should write a query to get the results you want. The query language used in the library assumes "and" as the comparison operator.

The amount of time a search takes depends on the size and organization of the database, the number of keywords you include in the query, and the comparison operator you use to join the keywords. An "or" search takes less time than an "and" search. In an "or" search, a document is considered a match as soon as any of the keywords is found. In an "and" search, a document is considered a match only if all the keywords are found, so the search engine must continue scanning the document until it finds every requested keyword.

To help people learn to do research on the Net, Anna created a small database that you can use to demonstrate searching on the Web. Although Yoko will be able to find some of the information she needs, she will need to use one of the Internet's large databases, such as Lycos, to find the rest. Using a search engine to query a larger database would return a much larger list of references than searching Anna's database will.

To conduct a query:

1. Return to the Peter H. Martin Library home page.

2. Click the **Research & Reference Section** link on the right side of the floor plan to connect to the Research & Reference Section page. See Figure 2-14.

Figure 2-14 ◄
Research &
Reference
Section page

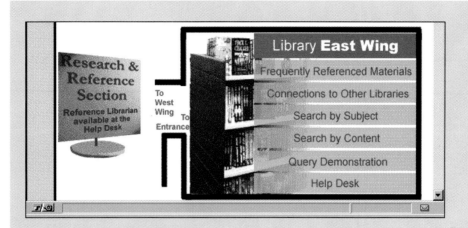

3. Click the **Query Demonstration** link to open the Query Form used in the library's demonstration. See Figure 2-15.

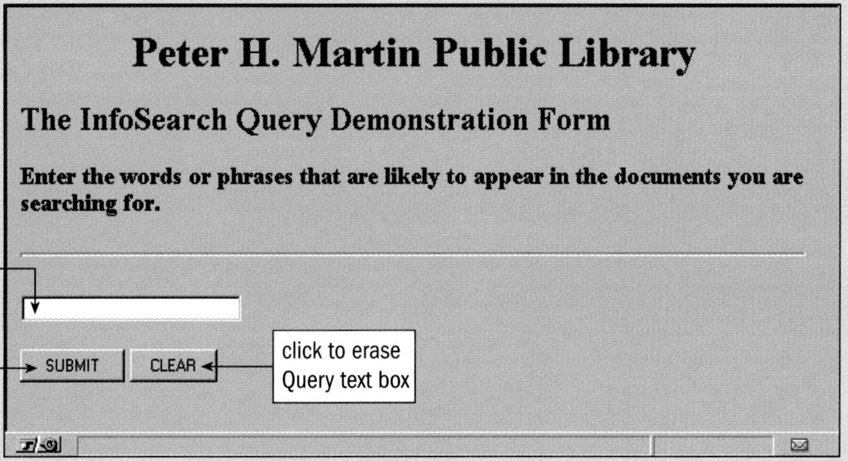

Figure 2-15 ◄
Query Form

Peter H. Martin Public Library

The InfoSearch Query Demonstration Form

Enter the words or phrases that are likely to appear in the documents you are searching for.

type query here ⟶

click to run query ⟶ ► SUBMIT ⬛ CLEAR ◄ ⟵ click to erase Query text box

4. Type **population statistics** in the Query text box to indicate the keywords you want to search for. The list of references returned will include any documents that contain both the words "population" *and* "statistics."

5. Click the **Submit** button to initiate the query search and compile a list of references. See Figure 2-16.

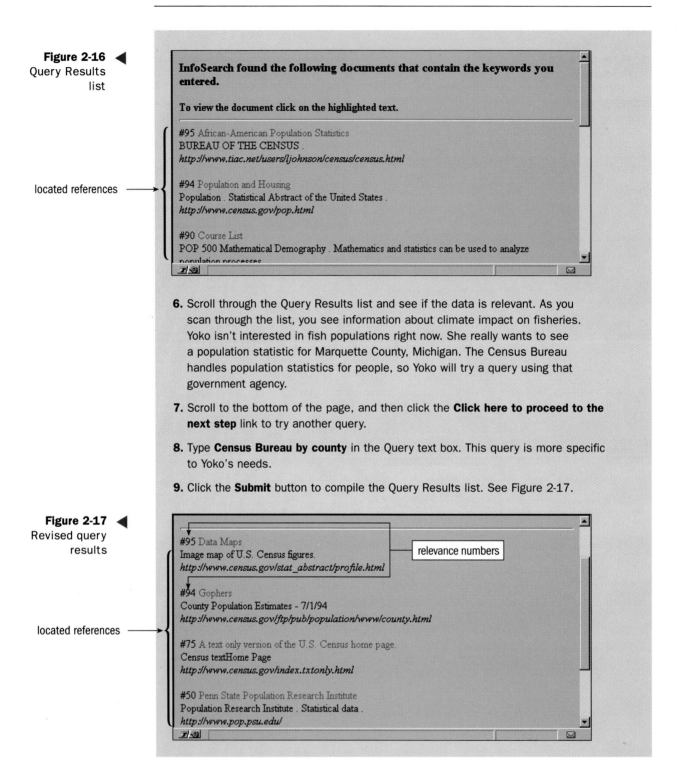

Figure 2-16
Query Results
list

located references

Figure 2-17
Revised query
results

located references

6. Scroll through the Query Results list and see if the data is relevant. As you scan through the list, you see information about climate impact on fisheries. Yoko isn't interested in fish populations right now. She really wants to see a population statistic for Marquette County, Michigan. The Census Bureau handles population statistics for people, so Yoko will try a query using that government agency.

7. Scroll to the bottom of the page, and then click the **Click here to proceed to the next step** link to try another query.

8. Type **Census Bureau by county** in the Query text box. This query is more specific to Yoko's needs.

9. Click the **Submit** button to compile the Query Results list. See Figure 2-17.

Although this query result seems more focused on Yoko's topic, it doesn't guarantee all the data will be relevant and useful. Most searches for keywords indicate the presence of those words in a document, rather than the context.

Determining Relevance

Although the list of references returned by a search contain the keywords in the query, those sites might not be in the proper context for what you want. You'll need to determine the relevance of the sites to your topic and ignore those that are unrelated.

The search engine orders the query results by their level of relevance, according to the methods chosen by the engine's developer. One such method is proximity of keywords within a document. In this method, when you submit a query on two or more keywords, a document is considered more relevant the closer these keywords are located to each other in the document. Some methods are more complex and accurate than others but can take longer to produce query results. The most relevant references to your query are at the top of the list and the least are the bottom of the list. In some search results, each reference is preceded by a numerical relevance rating, which can range from 100 (most relevant) to 0 (least relevant), for example.

Sometimes a query might be too general, which results in a large list of references that includes unrelated data. Other times, the query might be too specific and returns few or no references. In either case, you'll need to revise the query so that it is more or less inclusive, as necessary. Try adding adjectives or nouns that help focus the search or choosing synonyms that are more specific to your needs. Sometimes queries are case-sensitive, so capitalize any word that might be capitalized in references.

The fourth reference listed in Yoko's query results cites the U.S. Bureau of the Census housing statistics for Pennsylvania counties. With a relevance rating of 50, it matches the query but doesn't meet Yoko's needs at this point. The first and second references have high relevance factors, 95 and 94, and might lead her to the information she needs to answer her query. Yoko decides to check the Data Maps link first.

To check a site for relevance:

1. Click the **Data Maps** link in the first query reference to open the Census Bureau Data Maps for the U.S. See Figure 2-18.

Figure 2-18 ◀
State data map

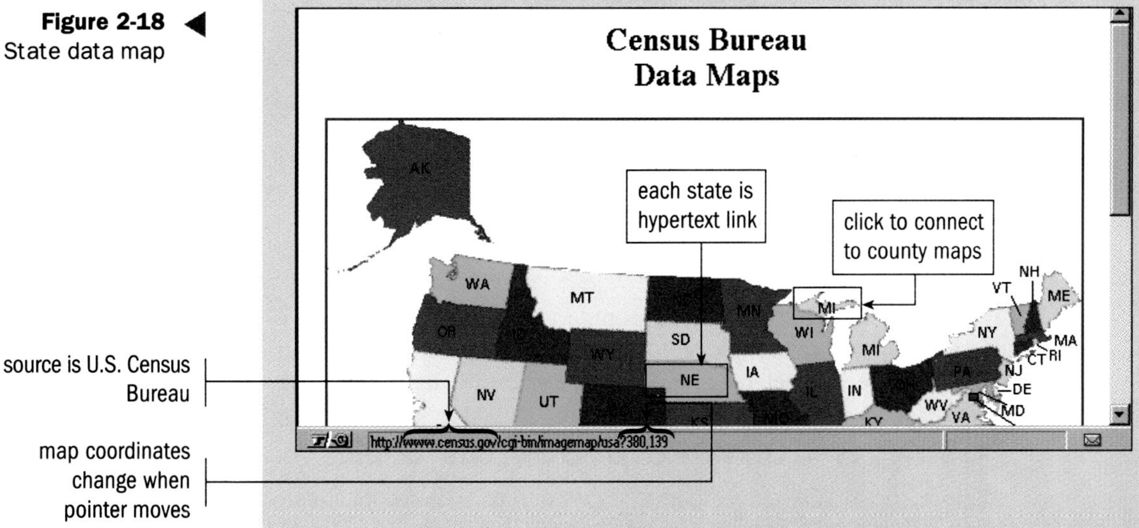

source is U.S. Census
Bureau

map coordinates
change when
pointer moves

TROUBLE? If the Data Maps site is busy, complete the next section "Using a Converted Gopher Site" and then try this set of steps again.

You'll need to click the top image for the state of Michigan and then Marquette County to find the population count.

2. Click the topmost MI image to open a map of counties in the Upper Peninsula of Michigan. Notice the links to related resources below the map. See Figure 2-19.

Figure 2-19 ◀
County data
map

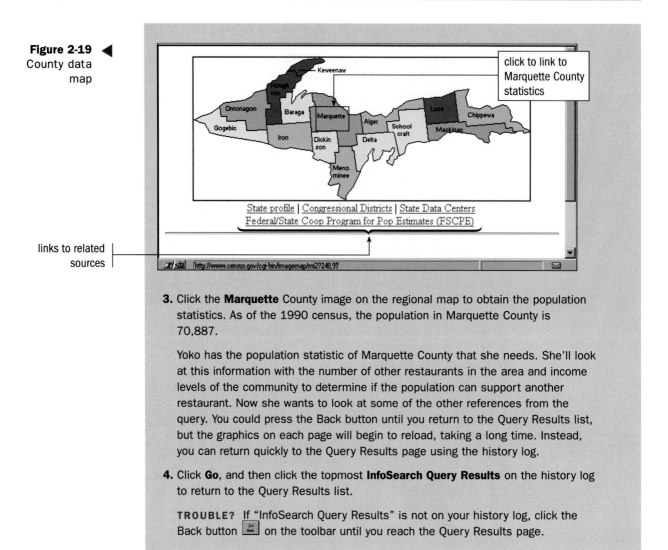

links to related
sources

3. Click the **Marquette** County image on the regional map to obtain the population statistics. As of the 1990 census, the population in Marquette County is 70,887.

Yoko has the population statistic of Marquette County that she needs. She'll look at this information with the number of other restaurants in the area and income levels of the community to determine if the population can support another restaurant. Now she wants to look at some of the other references from the query. You could press the Back button until you return to the Query Results list, but the graphics on each page will begin to reload, taking a long time. Instead, you can return quickly to the Query Results page using the history log.

4. Click **Go**, and then click the topmost **InfoSearch Query Results** on the history log to return to the Query Results list.

TROUBLE? If "InfoSearch Query Results" is not on your history log, click the Back button on the toolbar until you reach the Query Results page.

This site had some of the population information Yoko is looking for. The maps (graphics) made it simple to locate the data for Marquette County. Now Yoko wants to check the second reference on the Query Results list.

Using a Converted Gopher Site

Before the WWW existed, the University of Minnesota created Gophers to store and index text-based document files. **Gopher** is a protocol, like HTTP, but a Gopher uses menus to organize and search files on the Internet. The URL for every Gopher site begins "gopher://" just like the URL for every Web site begins "http://" Gophers provide a means for locating files by grouping them into directories, which you can access by opening nested menus. Nested menus work like file directories or folders; click the top-level menu to open a submenu, which can contain additional submenus or specific files about a topic. Continue to select various menus until you reach the file you want.

Gopher sites are entirely text-based, unlike Web pages, which can contain text, graphics, audio, and so on. As the WWW becomes more popular and widespread, the number of Gopher sites is diminishing, and many are converted to the HTTP protocol. When you connect to a Gopher site, you'll frequently find a message that the Gopher site is shutting down and reopening as a Web site. Similarly, if you encounter a Web page that is entirely text-based and contains little formatting, it probably was converted from a Gopher site.

Yoko wants to see what information is available at the second reference on the Query Results list. Although listed as Gopher, you can tell that the site was converted to a Web site because of the "http://" at the beginning of its URL.

To access a converted Gopher site:

1. Click **Gophers** in the second reference in the query results to connect to the list of states. Notice the screen format is much simpler than other Web sites you have visited. See Figure 2-20.

Figure 2-20 ◀
Converted
Gopher menu

text-based
menu items

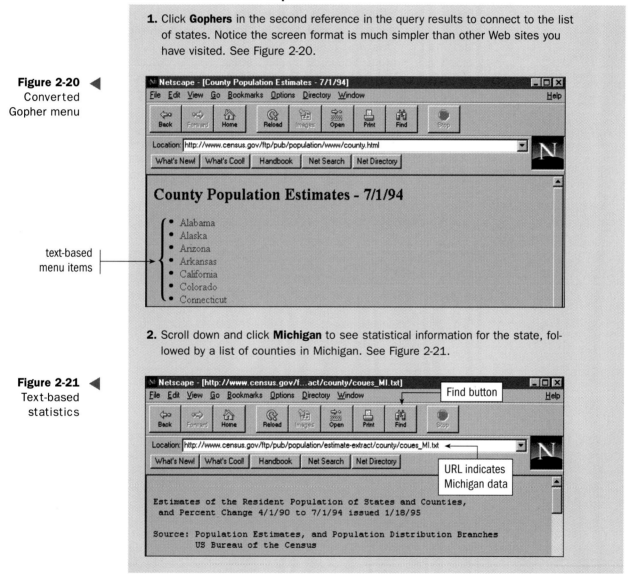

2. Scroll down and click **Michigan** to see statistical information for the state, followed by a list of counties in Michigan. See Figure 2-21.

Figure 2-21 ◀
Text-based
statistics

> **TROUBLE?** If you don't see the statistics for Michigan, you might not have selected the correct link. Click the Back button , and then repeat Step 2.

This page has so much text on it that it would be time-consuming to scroll the page and scan for the data Yoko wants. Instead, you use a Find command to search the document for a keyword.

Finding Words within a Document

Sometimes after you enter a query and follow a lead through several links, you'll end up with screens full of information. It is not always easy to find the relevant information, especially in lengthy text documents. You can scroll through the page and skim the text for data that matches your topic, but Netscape provides an easier way to locate text references—the Find tool. You enter a **search string**, which consists of words or phrases you want to locate in the document, in the Find dialog box. You can also tell Netscape to find only those words that match the capitalization you entered by selecting the Match case check box. Netscape highlights the first occurrence of the search string in the document and waits for you to decide if you want to look for any others. If Netscape doesn't find a match, a message dialog box opens to indicate the search string was not found. Make sure the spelling of the search string is correct and, if the Match case check box is checked, that the capitalization matches the case of the search string. If the search string is spelled correctly, try entering a different word or phrase.

Yoko wants to find out if Marquette County is included somewhere on the Michigan page without scanning the entire document. The Find tool does this task quickly.

REFERENCE window	USING FIND
	■ Click the Find button on the toolbar. ■ Type the word or phrase you want to locate in the Find what text box. ■ Click the Down radio button to search the document from the insertion point to the end of the document. ■ Click the Find Next button to locate the next occurrence of the word or phrase. ■ Click the Cancel button to close the dialog box.

To use the Find tool:

1. Click the **Find** button on the toolbar to open the Find dialog box.

   TROUBLE? If the toolbar is not visible, click Options, and then click Show Toolbar.

2. Type **Marquette** in the Find what text box.

3. Click the **Down** radio button to search from the insertion point to the end of the document.

4. Click the **Find Next** button in the Find dialog box. Netscape finds and highlights the first occurrence of "Marquette." See Figure 2-22.

Figure 2-22 ◀
Found text

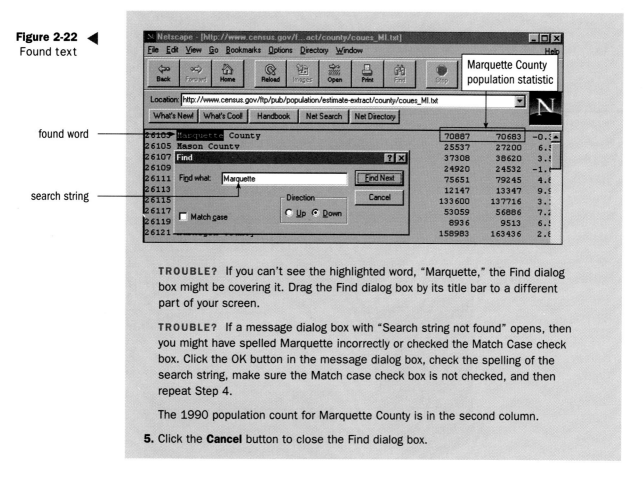

found word ——

search string ——

TROUBLE? If you can't see the highlighted word, "Marquette," the Find dialog box might be covering it. Drag the Find dialog box by its title bar to a different part of your screen.

TROUBLE? If a message dialog box with "Search string not found" opens, then you might have spelled Marquette incorrectly or checked the Match Case check box. Click the OK button in the message dialog box, check the spelling of the search string, make sure the Match case check box is not checked, and then repeat Step 4.

The 1990 population count for Marquette County is in the second column.

5. Click the **Cancel** button to close the Find dialog box.

Yoko has the population statistic she needs from the library's Query Demonstration. After she finds some other information about the number of competing restaurants and the average income for residents of the area, Yoko can determine if the local population can support another restaurant. However, remember that Anna assembled a smaller database to query as a demonstration. The same query of a larger database would yield a more comprehensive list of references and requires the more powerful search engine of a spider.

Searching with Spiders

A **spider** is indexing software that contains a search engine, a related database, and a document-retrieval system. A spider works by compiling a large index of existing Web pages on a database that you can search to find references to a specific subject. Sometimes called robot, harvester, or worm, the term *spider* has perhaps become the most popular one for indexing software because it extends the Web analogy. Figure 2-23 shows how the components of a spider work together.

Figure 2-23 ◀
How a spider
works

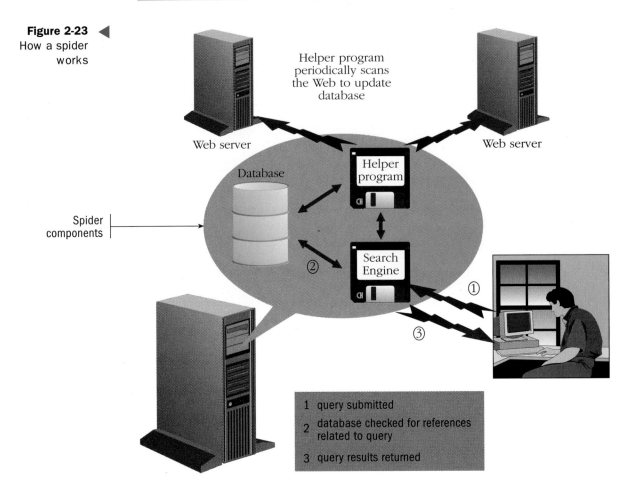

Helper program
periodically scans
the Web to update
database

Web server   Web server

Database

Spider
components

Helper
program

Search
Engine

②

①

③

1 query submitted

2 database checked for references
   related to query

3 query results returned

To understand how the spider creates a database, imagine a library that arranges its books randomly on the shelves and doesn't have a catalog index. The only way to locate information about any topic is to pick up a book and start reading and indexing it, jotting down keywords and references to other books. Follow these references and links until you reach a dead end, then repeat this process for all the other books in the library. The resulting list, in effect, is a database of the keywords and bibliography in each reference—a valuable way to locate all reference materials that relate to a keyword, such as Mozart. Now imagine adding to your list the books in all the libraries in your state, the country, and even the world. The resulting database, although time-consuming and tedious to compile, would yield even more information about a topic. A spider creates this type of database by circulating through millions of Web pages, one at a time, reading and storing keywords and links, until the links dead-end. The spider's helper programs organize the database by connecting some of the linked servers, removing duplicate entries, and categorizing the results.

Just as a library adds to its collection of books, new Web pages are added to the Internet at an astonishing rate. A spider periodically (daily or weekly) connects to servers throughout the Internet in order to update its database. When you submit a query to search a spider's database, the query results include only references that were available and within the spider's range when it last updated its database. If new Web pages are added since the last update or the spider couldn't access a Web page during an update, the index doesn't contain current references to them. If a Web page is not indexed in the database, it will not turn up in a search. So how can you ensure that you get the most current information available?

The enormous task of indexing the Internet is done by relatively few organizations. Spiders on the servers of these organizations take different, but overlapping, routes as they travel the Internet. Each one independently builds and maintains a database, so each database is built on different keywords. A query performed with the search engine of one spider usually provides a different result than asking the same query of another spider's database. To obtain a broad range of references that will more likely provide the data you need, use several spiders when researching a topic.

Anna compiled a list of popular spiders in the Research & Reference page. Yoko will use a spider to find additional Census information.

To use the search engine of a spider:

1. Click **Go**, and then click **Research & Reference Section** to return to the library's Research & Reference page.

   TROUBLE? If you don't see "Research & Reference Section" in the history log, click the Back button [Go Back] twice, and then click the Return to the end query demonstration link at the bottom of the page.

2. Click the **Search by Content** link on the Research & Reference page.

3. Click the **WebCrawler** link to connect to this popular Web search engine. See Figure 2-24.

Figure 2-24 ◀
WebCrawler
search tool

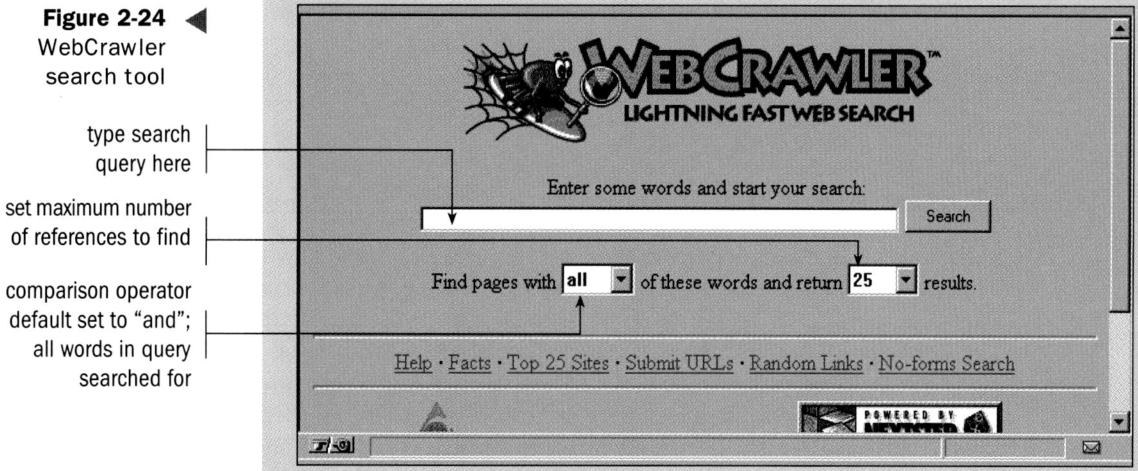

type search
query here

set maximum number
of references to find

comparison operator
default set to "and";
all words in query
searched for

4. Type **Census Bureau by county** in the Query text box, and then click the **Search** button. A Security Information dialog box opens, warning that the information you are sending (in this case, "Census Bureau by County") is not secure and that you shouldn't send any personal information, such as credit card numbers, that you want to keep private. Unless data you send is **encrypted**, or coded, it can be captured and read by anyone on the Internet. Netscape indicates sites that are secure sites by a solid key icon, rather than the broken key [icon] in the lower-left corner of your status bar.

   TROUBLE? If the Security Information dialog box does not open, then it might be disabled for your system. This site is still not secure, as indicated by the broken key icon, although the dialog box did not open.

5. If necessary, click the **Continue** button to close the Security Information dialog box and display the query results. See Figure 2-25. Your results will be different from those shown in Figure 2-25 because the database is constantly updated.

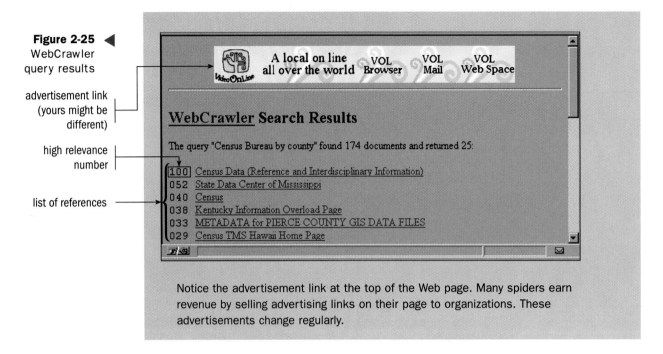

Figure 2-25
WebCrawler
query results

advertisement link
(yours might be
different)

high relevance
number

list of references

Notice the advertisement link at the top of the Web page. Many spiders earn
revenue by selling advertising links on their page to organizations. These
advertisements change regularly.

Netscape Communications Corporation compiles and maintains a list of popular
search tools on its Internet Search Web page, which you can open using the Net Search
directory button. These search tools work similarly to the WebCrawler, which you used
earlier. Netscape regularly updates the links on this page as more powerful or easier-to-
use search tools become available.

Searching by Subject

Sometimes when you begin studying a topic, you don't know what keywords to use in a
content search. Instead, you can search for applicable information by subject. The navigational guides you used earlier for surfing also can be used to search by subject. These lists
are organized first by general and then successively more specific subjects as you search.

Yoko knows that many new businesses fail within a short time, due in part to lack of
planning and knowledge of where and how to get resources. Because her restaurant will
be a small business, she thinks the government might provide funding or consulting assistance at the federal, state, or local level. She wants to know all her options but isn't sure
where to begin looking. A subject search using a navigational guide is a good starting
point. The Research & Reference Section Web page contains a link to some of these
subject guides.

To search by subject with a navigational guide:

1. Click **Go**, and then click the lower **Research & Reference Section** to return to
   the Research & Reference page.

2. Click the **Search by Subject** link.

3. Click the **Yahoo** link (or any one of the other hypertext links if Yahoo is busy) to
   access an Internet subject guide. See Figure 2-26.

Most of these guides work similarly, so follow these steps for any of the guides. If you are using a guide other than Yahoo, the Web pages you see will differ slightly from the figures in this set of steps.

Figure 2-26 ◀
Subject guide

main category ——

included topics ——

click to find business topics —

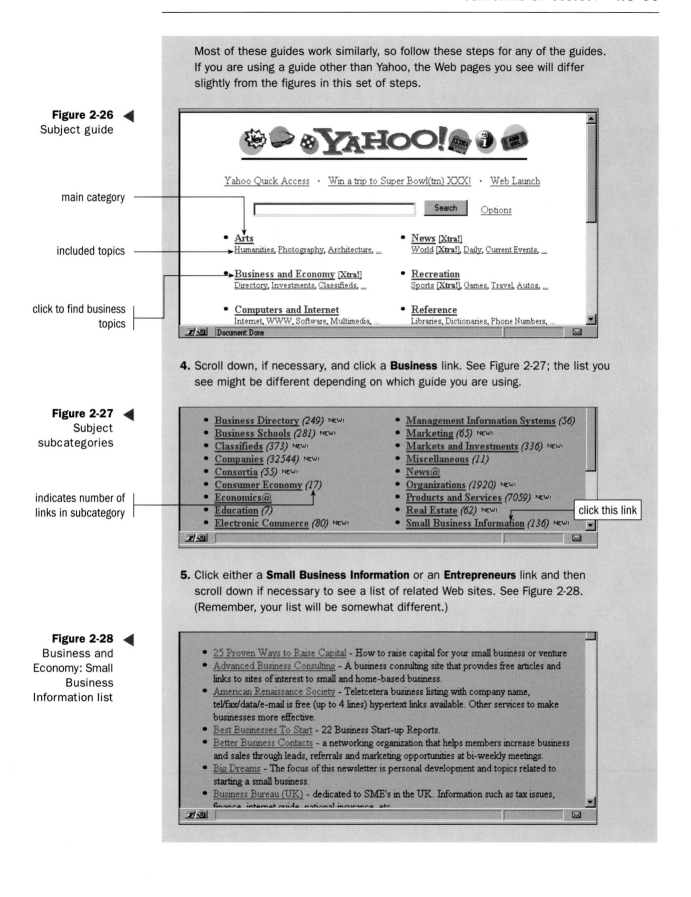

4. Scroll down, if necessary, and click a **Business** link. See Figure 2-27; the list you see might be different depending on which guide you are using.

Figure 2-27 ◀
Subject subcategories

indicates number of links in subcategory

5. Click either a **Small Business Information** or an **Entrepreneurs** link and then scroll down if necessary to see a list of related Web sites. See Figure 2-28. (Remember, your list will be somewhat different.)

Figure 2-28 ◀
Business and Economy: Small Business Information list

Yoko has many topics to investigate to increase her knowledge about small business opportunities.

6. Click a **Small Business Administration** or related link to follow up one of the references.

Yoko comments that because such a wealth of material is available about small businesses, she'll never be able to read it all before the library closes. Printing all these Web pages will require a lot of paper and time. You suggest that she save the pages she wants to look at to a disk.

Saving Text and Images to a File

Saving Web pages to a disk not only saves you paper and the time it would take to print the pages; it also reduces the amount of time you spend online. This can save you a lot of money if you pay a connection charge for using an online service provider. If the fee is charged per minute of connection time, reading Web pages online can become very costly.

You can save a Web page to disk with or without the images. When Netscape saves an HTML format as a text file, only the text is saved in a simple font. All the images, special fonts, links, and color are not saved. If the Web page contains a lot of graphics with important content, you will no longer be able to see or use that information. Determine if a Web page you want to save will be helpful when the graphics are not included.

Alternatively, you can save a Web page as an .html file. The saved file will look similar to the Web page, including all the special fonts and colors. However, you will be able to read the file only with Netscape or another Web browser (although you don't need to be connected to the Internet) because the file is a coded **source document,** a file embedded with special characters. Word-processing programs will be unable to interpret the HTML codes, making the text harder to read.

Saving a Web Page as a Text File

Yoko wants to save the Web page about the Small Business Association that she is reading.

REFERENCE
window

SAVING A WEB PAGE AS TEXT

- Click File, and then click Save as.
- Type the filename in the File name text box.
- Click the Save as type list arrow, and then click Plain Text (.txt).
- Click the Save button.

To save the current Web page as a text file:

1. Insert your Student Disk into drive A or the appropriate drive on your computer.

2. Click **File**, and then click **Save as** to open the Save As dialog box.

TROUBLE? If the Save as command is dimmed, you might not have finished loading the entire Web document. Click the Reload button 🖳 on the toolbar to reload the Web page.

3. Click the **Save as type** list arrow to see the file type options.

4. Click **Plain text (*.txt)** in the Save as type list box so the Web page is saved as readable text rather than as HTML coding.

5. Click the **File name** text box, and then type **a:\tut2-2** to name the file being created. See Figure 2-29.

Figure 2-29 ◀
Save As dialog
box

type filename here —

click to change
file type

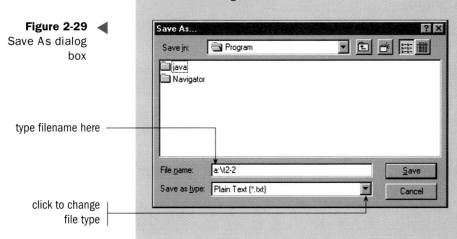

6. Press the **Enter** key to close the dialog box and save the file to your disk.

Before Yoko saves any more pages, she should double-check that the page saved properly.

Opening a Text File in Netscape

Because you saved the document as a text file, you could open and edit it with any word-processing program. You can also open the file from Netscape, but only for viewing purposes.

You'll open Yoko's file from within Netscape to verify that it saved properly.

REFERENCE
window

OPENING A TEXT FILE FROM WITHIN NETSCAPE

■ Click File, and then click Open File.
■ Select Text (*.txt) file format from the Files of type text box.
■ Double-click the filename you want to open.

To open a file:

1. Click **File**, and then click **Open File**. The Open dialog box opens.

2. Click the **Files of type** list arrow, and then click **Text (*.txt)** to display the tut2-2 file you just saved in the file list. See Figure 2-30.

Figure 2-30 ◀
Open dialog
box

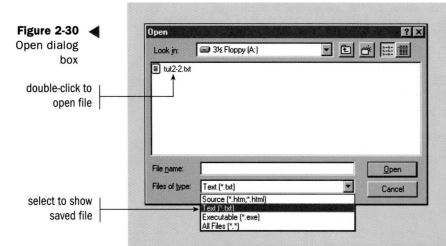

double-click to
open file

select to show
saved file

TROUBLE? If tut2-2 doesn't appear in the file list, you might be looking in the wrong drive or at the wrong file type. Make sure the Look in text box lists "3½ Floppy (A:)" or the appropriate drive. Make sure the Files of type text box shows "Text (*.txt)." If you still can't find the file, repeat the steps in the section "Saving a Web Page as a Text File."

3. Double-click **tut2-2** to open the file in the Netscape page content area. Notice that you saved only the text of the Web page. See Figure 2-31.

Figure 2-31 ◀
Viewing a
text file

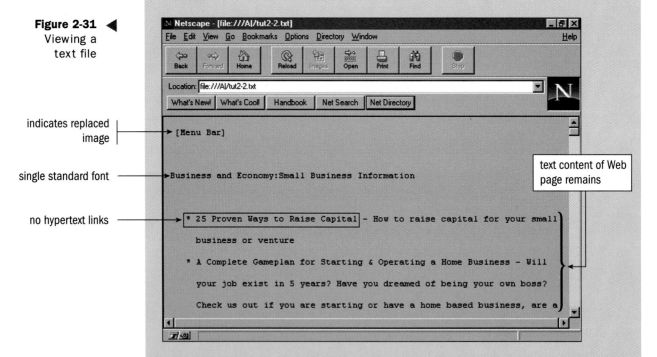

indicates replaced
image

single standard font

no hypertext links

text content of Web
page remains

TROUBLE? If your text file looks *exactly* like your Web page, including all the special fonts, you did not save the document as a Text file and you won't be able to open it in a word-processing program. Repeat the steps in the section "Saving a Web Page as a Text File," and then click the Yes button in the message dialog box if asked if you want to replace the existing file named tut2-2.

4. Click **Go**, and then click the lower **Research & Reference Section** to return to the library's Research & Reference Section page.

Yoko mentions that she might want to use a graphic from a Web page on her promotional material. You suggest that she save a graphic from the library's Web pages so she can see how to save images.

Saving an Image from a Web page

Although Web page images aren't saved to a file along with the text, you can save images as separate files.

Image files can be saved in a variety of file formats. The two most common image files are .GIF and .JPEG. As with audio files, the difference between the types of file is image quality and file size. You'll also need software that can interpret these different image file types if you want to view and use them.

You'll save an image from the library's Web page for Yoko.

REFERENCE window

SAVING AN IMAGE FROM A WEB PAGE

- Position the pointer over the image you want to copy, and then click the right mouse button.
- Click Save this Image as on the shortcut menu.
- Type a filename in the File name text box.
- Click the Save as type list arrow, and then click GIF Files (*.gif).
- Press the Enter key.

To save an image from a Web page:

1. Position your pointer over the **Library East Wing** image; you might need to scroll to see it.

2. Click the *right* mouse button to open a shortcut menu. See Figure 2-32.

Figure 2-32 ◄
Shortcut menu

click to open
Save As
dialog box

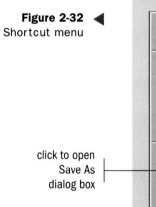

Back
Forward

Open this (east.map?189,-284)
Add Bookmark for this Link
New Window with this Link
Save this Link as...
Copy this Link Location

View this Image (imapr.gif)
➤Save this Image as...
Copy this Image Location
Load this Image

Internet Shortcut

3. Click **Save this Image as** to open the Save As dialog box.

4. Type **a:\image** in the File name text box to name a file on your disk.

5. Make sure that GIF File (*.gif) appears in the Save as type text box, and then press the Enter key. The Save As dialog box closes, and the image is saved to your disk.

   Now you'll open the file in Netscape and view the image to verify that it saved properly.

6. Click **File**, and then click **Open File**. The Open dialog box opens.

7. Click the **Files of type** list arrow, and then click **All Files (*)** to display the entire contents of your disk.

8. Double-click **image.gif** to close the Open dialog box and view the saved .GIF image in the Netscape page content area.

TROUBLE? If you do not see image.gif in the Open dialog box, you might be looking in the wrong drive or at the wrong file type. Make sure the Look in text box lists "3½ Floppy (A:)" or the appropriate drive. Make sure the Files of type text box shows "All Files (*)." If you still can't find the file, repeat Steps 1 through 8.

Yoko saves a number of documents that have information about starting a small business. She also finds several drawings and other graphics that she thinks would be great to use on her promotional materials and saves those to her disk. She wants to know if she can legally reproduce these graphics on her take-out menu and advertisements.

Reproducing Material from the Internet

As you've just seen, reproducing text and images from Internet sites around the world is easy to do, perhaps even easier than photocopying. The quality of the copied material is the same as the original; colors, shading, and graphics do not darken or distort, as they might in a photocopy. This makes it simple to copy an image or text from the Internet and reproduce it for personal, academic, or commercial use. However, similar to those for printed material, restrictions apply to the use of these files.

All printed material, such as books and magazines, and all audio material, such as music CDs or books on tape, are protected from unlimited reproduction by copyright law. A **copyright** is a federal law that allows an author (or the copyright holder) to control how his or her work is used, including how the material is reproduced, sold or distributed, adapted, and performed or displayed. As soon as the author's original words, music, drawing, photograph, and so forth is in a tangible form (on paper, cassette, electronic file, and so forth), the work is copyrighted whether or not it carries a copyright notice (for example, © 1998 Anna Ferri). A copyright protects the way ideas and facts are presented, but not the ideas and facts themselves.

Depending on how much material you want to reproduce from the Internet and your purpose in reproducing it, you might need to get permission from the Web page owner (the copyright holder) and, in some cases, pay a fee. Figure 2-33 outlines some guidelines for determining when you need to request permission before reusing material from the Internet. Remember that people, authors and artists, have made their works available over an electronic medium for increased distribution, not for increased duplication.

Figure 2-33 ◄
Guidelines for reusing material from the Internet

Copyright Notice	Academic Use (term paper, research paper, class materials)	Commercial Use (advertisement, will be copyrighted, will be sold)
Copyrighted	Can reuse certain amount without permission. Include proper citation. Request permission to reuse large amounts.	Request permission from page owner.
No copyright or mention of use	Assume copyrighted.	Assume copyrighted.
Source states "use freely no restrictions"	Can reuse without permission.	Can reuse without permission.

Because the copyright law was last revised in 1978, long before widespread use of the Internet, there are many gray areas in how to properly reproduce and reuse electronic and multimedia materials available on the Internet. The guidelines for using copyrighted material, called Fair Use, are still being developed for the Net. For accurate information, ask someone knowledgeable about the Internet and copyright laws, such as personnel at large or university libraries who have undergone training.

USES AND
abuses

COPYING MATERIAL FROM THE INTERNET

Remembering a few guidelines about copying and reproducing material from Web pages, such as text and images, will help ensure that you respect the author's copyright.

- Appropriate academic use only by students and faculty.
- Use a limited amount of text or number of images from one source.
- Always include a proper citation.
- Commercial use requires permission.
- If in doubt, request permission.

More and more of the library's visitors have been asking about how copyrights apply to the Internet. To help the library staff field some of the most common questions, Anna added a Help Desk to the Research & Reference Section page with answers to some copyright issues. You'll show these to Yoko.

To reference a list of copyright guidelines:

1. If necessary, return to the Research & Reference Section page.

2. Click the **Help Desk** link to see the list of guidelines Anna put on the Web page. See Figure 2-34.

Figure 2-34 ◀
Citation and
Fair Use
references

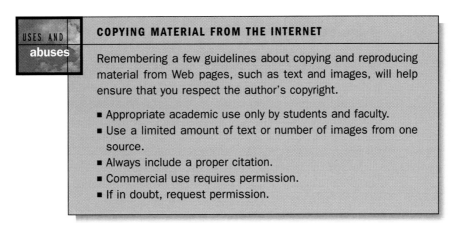

Help Desk

- APA -- The American Psychological Association publication style guide online.
- Fair Use -- Discusses the fair use provisions of the Copyright Law.
- Citation Style -- Offers guidelines and samples for citing Internet sources in academic papers.
- Purdue On-Line Writing Lab -- Online tutorial center for writers provides detailed information about grammar, source citations, ESL, writing resumes and papers, and more.

[HOME] [LIBRARY ENTRANCE] [BROWSING SECTION] [COMMENTS]

Document: Done

3. Click the **APA** link to see an example of a correct bibliographic citation for electronic media. As an example, the citation for the Research & Reference Section page content is:

Poindexter, S. (1996) *Research & Reference Section Page.*[Online].
Available: http://www.vmedia.com/cti/NewPerspectives/tiun/t2b.html.

4. Click the **Back** button on the toolbar and return to the Help Desk.

5. Click the **Fair Use** link to read about what material you can reuse without obtaining permission from the Web page owner.

Yoko can reuse a graphic from the Internet in some instances. If she were writing a research paper on starting a Japanese take-out restaurant, she could include the graphic with its citation. Because she wants to use the graphic in a commercial setting for her own profit, Yoko needs to request permission from its creator to use the graphic.

Copying Material to the Clipboard

Just as with any other copyrighted material you reproduce, you should record any available bibliography information for material from the Internet. You could just write down the bibliographic material with pen and paper, but it's easier to copy the listing to the clipboard and then paste it in a word-processing document. This way, you can ensure that the spelling and other information remains accurate.

Because Yoko might want to use material from the Fair Use page, she copies the bibliographic material first into the clipboard and then into a word-processing program.

To copy to the clipboard:

1. Click the **location** box to highlight the URL of the current page.

2. Click **Edit**. See Figure 2-35.

Figure 2-35 ◀
Copying to
clipboard

click to copy URL
to clipboard

highlighted selection

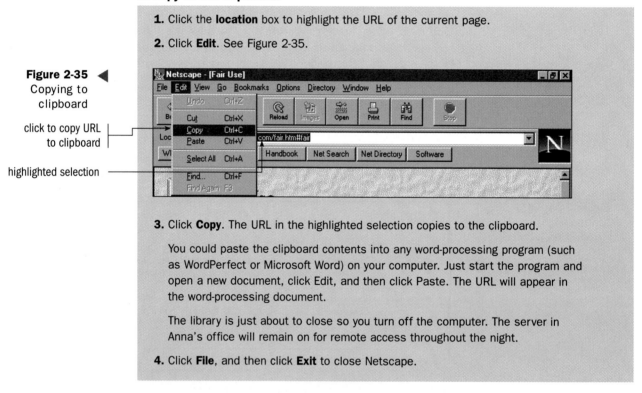

3. Click **Copy**. The URL in the highlighted selection copies to the clipboard.

You could paste the clipboard contents into any word-processing program (such as WordPerfect or Microsoft Word) on your computer. Just start the program and open a new document, click Edit, and then click Paste. The URL will appear in the word-processing document.

The library is just about to close so you turn off the computer. The server in Anna's office will remain on for remote access throughout the night.

4. Click **File**, and then click **Exit** to close Netscape.

Yoko is pleased with all the information she has gathered and what she has learned about researching on the Internet. She still needs to find more information about opening her restaurant before she can decide on her business plans. You assure Yoko that you will be one of her first customers if she does open her take-out restaurant.

Quick Check

1. You submit database queries to a _____ to search the Web for keywords.

2. In a query, which comparison operator, "or" or "and," results in more site references? Why?

3. True or False: All sites listed in a query result are relevant to the user's needs.

4. Many text-based _____ sites are being converted to Web pages to take advantage of formatting and graphics.

5. _____ are computer software that periodically index Web page contents and URLs into topics for use in query searches.

6. When you don't know keywords to use for a search, use a _____ guide to search for general topics.

7. Web pages can be saved as _____ files, opened in a word-processing document, and read offline.

8. True or False: You can insert one .GIF image, copied from the Internet, into a college term paper without requesting permission from the Web page owner.

Tutorial Assignments

Yoko Muramoto is continuing with her plans to open a take-out restaurant serving Japanese food, and she regularly checks the Web for new and useful sites that might help her. She is particularly interested in any page that deals with Michigan, small businesses, the restaurant business, or Japanese culture.

Right now Yoko wants additional information about insurance for her business. She learned from other small business owners that the Michigan Insurance Bureau provides information specially geared to small businesses. She thinks they might have a Web page. Yoko also wants to find Web pages for other businesses that deal with Japanese food. She asks you to find the Web page for the Michigan Insurance Bureau and Web pages dealing with Japanese food, recipes, or restaurants.

If necessary, start Netscape, and then do the following:

1. Open the Web page at the URL "http://www.vmedia.com/cti/NewPerspectives/tiun."
2. Click the Tutorial Assignments and Case Problems link.
3. Scroll down until you see the Tutorial 2 Tutorial Assignments.
4. Click the Search by Content link at the Peter H. Martin Library Research & Reference Section.
5. Click the WebCrawler link.
6. Enter "Michigan Insurance Bureau" in the Query text box and press Enter.
7. E-mail the list of sites returned by WebCrawler to your instructor using the Mail Document command on the File menu. In the e-mail message, indicate which site is the most relevant. Using the relevance numbers, indicate how the first site compares to the second, based on those numbers.

8. Is a link to the Michigan Insurance Bureau shown? If so, click that link and then save a copy of the Michigan Insurance Bureau page to a text file. If not, connect to a link for the state or government of Michigan and look further for the Insurance site. If there is not a link to the Michigan Insurance Bureau, save the current page to a text file.
9. Use the history log to return to the Research & Reference Section page.

10. Link to a different spider on the Search by Content list, and type the "Michigan Insurance Bureau" query again. How do the results differ?
11. Return to the Research & Reference Section page using the history log, and then click the Search by Subject link.

12. Click the Yahoo link.
13. Proceed through the more detailed levels of entertainment and foods subjects to find a list of Web pages related to Japanese food by clicking appropriate links.
14. Open a Web page related to Japanese food.
15. Click Windows, then click Bookmarks.
16. Open the Bookmarks file on your Student Disk.
17. Open three additional Japanese Web pages and add a bookmark to your bookmark file for each site.
18. E-mail one Japanese food site to your instructor using the Mail Document command on the File menu. In the message of the e-mail, indicate why you chose this site.

Case Problems

1. Sightseeing with LaFrancois Travel Danielle LaFrancois, owner and chief agent at the LaFrancois Travel Agency, uses the Web to keep tabs on various festivals and activities taking place at tourist sites around the country. She recently learned of some inexpensive airfare to Edinburgh, the capital of Scotland. The tickets will be available at that price for only a short time so she wants to find some current information on Edinburgh and Glasgow, a nearby city, to help encourage people to purchase the tickets. She asks you to use the Web to find the following information for both cities: what activities are happening; a list of museums and galleries; and some other places of interest.

If necessary, launch Netscape, then do the following:

1. Open the Web page at the URL "http://www.vmedia.com/cti/NewPerspectives/tiun" and then click the Tutorial Assignments and Case Problems link.
2. Scroll down until you see the Tutorial 2 Case Problems section.
3. Click the Travel Logs link in the Browsing Section of the Peter H. Martin Library.
4. Open the Fodor's link and add a bookmark for that page to your bookmark file.

5. Navigate through the maps of Europe to locate information about Edinburgh. Save any information you find on the Edinburgh page to a text file.
6. Return to the Travel Logs in the Browsing Section page using the history log.

7. Investigate Glasgow using the Virtual Tourist II or City.Net links. *Hint*: Follow the United Kingdom links under Europe.
8. Mail the Glasgow document to your instructor. Write a short note in the message content area of the e-mail stating whether you think Glasgow or Edinburgh offer the better tourist attractions at this time.

9. Open the previously saved Fodor's text file using word-processing program (such as Wordpad or Notepad), type your name at the top, and print the file.

2. Reading the news from Halifax Halifax, a city in Nova Scotia, Canada, northeast of Maine, is situated along the Atlantic Ocean and fishing is a major industry. In recent years, it has flourished also as a tourist town thanks to the natural beauty of the area. David Wu wants to spend his summer working at one of the fishing resorts in the area. Before he can pack his bags, he wants to learn a little more about daily living in Halifax. He asks you to use the Web to get the headlines from a Halifax newspaper, find out about the climate, and determine popular sporting events in Halifax.

If necessary, launch Netscape, then do the following:

1. Open the Web page at the URL "http://www.vmedia.com/cti/NewPerspectives/tiun" and then click the Tutorial Assignments and Case Problems link.
2. Scroll down until you see the Tutorial 2 Case Problems section, click the Newspapers and Magazines link in the Browsing Section of the Peter H. Martin Library.

3. Follow either the Yahoo's Guide to Media link or the Newspapers on the Net link to reach a listing of newspapers published on the Internet.
4. Locate one of the Halifax newspapers using Netscape's Find command.
5. Connect to the newspaper and add a bookmark to your bookmark file.
6. Navigate through the pages to obtain the information about today's weather and a local sporting event that David wants.
7. When you have all the information, prepare to e-mail the page containing the headlines of a Halifax newspaper to your instructor using the Mail Document command.
8. In the message of the e-mail, briefly summarize the facts you gathered and then send the e-mail message.

3. Job Searching on the Web Keisha Williams, a senior at MidWest University, is actively searching for employment in marketing, her major field of study. She'd like to move to Texas. She asks you to help her use the Web to locate resources for job searches and find some tips on writing resumes. One popular site to find job listings is the CareerMosaic home page, which contains the J.O.B.S. database that you can use to search for specific jobs in different parts of the country. Unfortunately, you don't know the address of the site, so you'll have to find the Web page before you can search for job listings. The J.O.B.S. Database page contains several fields into which you can enter the information specific to the job you're seeking.

If necessary, launch Netscape, then do the following:

1. Use the Net Search directory button to open a list of spider search engines.
2. Select one search engine and type "CareerMosaic" or "Career Magazine" in the Query text box, and then submit the query as indicated by the search engine.

3. Scroll through the list of sites returned by the query until you see relevant page referrals.
4. Connect to the CareerMosaic or Career Magazine home page.
5. Using the search criteria given by Keisha, look for available positions. In Keisha's case, you should search for jobs related to marketing and limit the search to jobs in Texas. If you don't find any in Texas, expand your search to nearby states.
6. Connect to a link that describes a job you think is appropriate for Keisha.
7. E-mail the job description page to your instructor using the Mail Document command.
8. Use the history log to return to the home page of the search engine you used earlier.

9. Search for pages that contain resume writing tips.
10. Investigate the pages that seem the most helpful. Select the one that looks like the best resource and save it to your disk as a text file.

4. Scavenger Hunt on the World Wide Web Now that you've had some experience using search tools on the WWW, you should be able to locate almost any type of information on the Web. Complete the following "scavenger hunt"; use any tool available at the Peter H. Martin Library. As you find an answer write it down.

If necessary, launch Netscape, then do the following:

1. Open the Web page at the URL "http://www.vmedia.com/cti/NewPerspectives/tiun" and then click the Tutorial 2 link.

2. In what Shakespearean play does a character say "There's no trust, no faith, no honesty in men; all perjured, all forsworn, all naught, all dissemblers" (specify the act and the scene)? *Hint*: Look for The Shakespeare Home Page, which contains a tool for searching the contents of all Shakespeare's plays and poems.

3. In the movie "Three Little Words," who played the part of Harry Ruby? *Hint*: Look for The Internet Movie Database page and then use a search tool to find a movie titled "Three Little Words."

4. What is the current temperature, humidity, wind and barometric pressure at Caribou, Maine? *Hint*: Look for a page that deals with weather in the Travel Logs section of the Peter H. Martin Library home page.

5. What is the address, phone number and e-mail address of your congressional representative in the U.S. House of Representatives? *Hint*: Use the Yahoo index to search for government resources.

6. What is the current estimate of the population of the United States and of the world? *Hint*: Use the Planet Earth Home Page in the Browsing Section of the Peter H. Martin Library home page.

7. What is the ZIP code for Nome, Alaska (abbreviated AK)? *Hint*: Check the Frequently Used References at the Peter H. Martin Library.

8. What is the URL for the Smithsonian Institute's home page?

9. When you have found the answers to all the above, send an e-mail message to your instructor with the answers in the message content area.

Corresponding with E-mail and Transferring Files

Providing Technical Support for Global Marketers, Inc.

OBJECTIVES

In this tutorial you will:

- Use the e-mail function
- Send and receive e-mail messages
- Create an Address Book
- Send and receive e-mail attachments
- Read, reply to, and forward e-mail messages
- Save messages for future reference
- Delete e-mail messages and Address Book entries
- Download uncompression software using FTP
- Run a virus scan on downloaded software
- Download compressed shareware using FTP
- Uncompress and run downloaded shareware

LABS

E-Mail

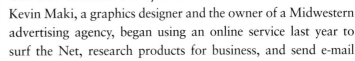

Global Marketers, Inc.

CASE Kevin Maki, a graphics designer and the owner of a Midwestern advertising agency, began using an online service last year to surf the Net, research products for business, and send e-mail messages to friends and clients. He realized the enormous potential for commercial development on the World Wide Web (WWW).

The WWW attracts thousands of people daily, each of whom is a potential customer. These potential customers choose which Web sites they want to visit, including commercial companies trying to market a product or service. In other words, people visit a site to find information about a product they are interested in, rather than the company having to locate them. At commercial sites, customers can focus on their interests and look at only the Web pages that most appeal to them. The company and product information is available 24 hours a day anywhere in the world, not just to a selected audience that happens to be watching a specific television show or walking past a certain billboard. For example, when a user in Wyoming turns on a computer at 8 p.m. and connects to a computer in Amsterdam, where it is almost dawn, there is no indication that the linked computer is thousands of miles away in another time zone. This ability of the WWW to transcend time and distance boundaries encourages a global economy.

While attending an international technology conference for graphic designers, Kevin met Megan Wolfe of Germany and Jane Phillips of England. Both women, leading partners in their advertising agencies, were interested in pursuing a joint venture. After much planning and negotiation, they recently merged their respective independent agencies to form Global Marketers, Inc. The company offers online advertising consulting, part of the expanding field of Internet marketing. The partners expect the business to grow quickly as more and more companies advertise their products on the Net.

Kevin needs to make sure that he is able to contact his partners in England and Germany and that he can send and receive files from either office. He asks you to make sure his e-mail system is set up and working properly and that he can transfer files from both overseas offices and any clients to his computer.

In this session, you will use Netscape's e-mail function to send and receive e-mail messages and attachments; create an address file; and save and delete messages.

E-Mail

Using the E-mail Function

As more people connect to the Internet and have access to e-mail programs, communicating by e-mail is becoming increasingly popular and more prevalent. **E-mail**, or electronic mail, is the transfer of messages between hosts on the Internet. People use e-mail for both business and personal communication. When you need to send information to someone else, an e-mail message can save time and money because you don't need to wait for expensive postal delivery nor do you need to make expensive long-distance phone calls. You can send e-mail to and receive e-mail from anyone in the world who has an e-mail address, regardless of the operating system and type of computer they are using.

An e-mail address consists of a **user ID** (the user name), the @ symbol, and a host name (the domain address). For example, the e-mail address for the President of the United States is:

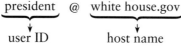

Like URLs, every e-mail address is unique. Many people might use the same host, but their user IDs distinguish one e-mail address from another.

The time it takes to send an e-mail depends on the size of the message, the speed of your modem, and the level of Internet traffic at that time. When you send an e-mail, your local server examines the host name. Messages addressed to people at the same host site as the person sending the e-mail are processed and distributed without connecting to the Internet. Messages addressed to people at other host sites are sent out over the Internet. Because the Internet is so vast, your local mail server is not connected to every other host, so e-mail is rarely sent along a direct path to the recipient. Instead, the message is handed from one host to another until the e-mail reaches its destination. Figure 3-1 shows how the Internet routes an e-mail message from a student at the University of Alaska to a student at the University of the Virgin Islands.

Figure 3-1 ◀
Internet e-mail
routes

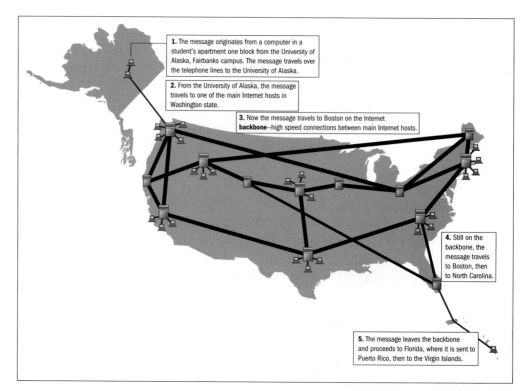

1. The message originates from a computer in a student's apartment one block from the University of Alaska, Fairbanks campus. The message travels over the telephone lines to the University of Alaska.

2. From the University of Alaska, the message travels to one of the main Internet hosts in Washington state.

3. Now the message travels to Boston on the Internet **backbone**—high speed connections between main Internet hosts.

4. Still on the backbone, the message travels to Boston, then to North Carolina.

5. The message leaves the backbone and proceeds to Florida, where it is sent to Puerto Rico, then to the Virgin Islands.

The first thing Kevin asks you to do is get information from the New Perspectives on the Internet Using Netscape Navigator page. The site is set up so that you enter your e-mail address, and the site automatically returns a message. Kevin would like to see a copy of the information the company sends. He also mentions that you can open a Web page by typing the URL directly into the Location text box, rather than opening the Open Location dialog box.

To have a message sent to you automatically:

1. If necessary, launch Netscape.

2. Click the **Location** text box to highlight the current URL.

3. Type **http://www.vmedia.com/cti/NewPerspectives/tiun**, then press the **Enter** key to open the New Perspectives on the Internet Using Netscape Navigator page.

4. Click the **Tutorial 3** link, then click the Generating **E-mail** link to open the Generating E-mail page.

5. Type your full e-mail address in the text box, including the host name after the @ symbol.

   TROUBLE? If you don't know your user e-mail address, ask your instructor or technical support person for help.

6. Click the **Submit** button to have an e-mail message sent to you. You will read this e-mail message later.

You want to ensure that all three branches of Global Marketers are communicating online effectively and quickly. Each branch office is connected to the Internet through a local service provider and has e-mail capability, but not everyone uses the same program. Kevin already uses Netscape as his Web browser so you suggest that he use it as his e-mail program as well. This way, when he's connected to the Internet he won't have to switch programs to read or send e-mail messages; everything can be done from within Netscape.

Configuring Netscape for the E-mail Function

Before you can use the Netscape e-mail function, you must make sure it is **configured**, or set up, properly by checking the Netscape preferences. Netscape needs the address of your local Internet servers, your name, and your e-mail address before you can use its e-mail function. Your e-mail information is included in every e-mail message you send, both as an identifier and as a return address. Two servers work together to traffic your outgoing and incoming messages. **SMTP** (Simple Mail Transport Protocol) is the method servers use to handle outgoing messages. Incoming e-mail is handled by a **POP** (Post Office Protocol) server that connects to your local network. Though typically the same, the POP and SMTP server names can be different.

You'll begin by making sure your e-mail servers and personal identification are configured correctly.

To configure the preferences for e-mail messages:

1. Click **Options**, then click **Mail and News Preferences** to open the Preferences dialog box.

2. Click the **Servers** tab in the dialog box. See Figure 3-2.

Figure 3-2 ◀
Mail server
preferences

type names supplied
by your network
administrator

type your full
e-mail address

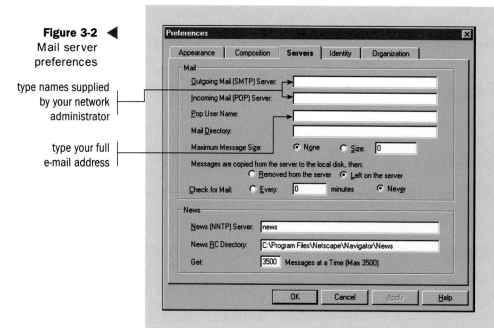

3. If the Outgoing Mail (SMTP) Server text box and the Incoming Mail (POP) Server text box are blank, ask your instructor or technical support person what to enter in them.

Before the POP server can check whether you received any mail, it must know what name to look for.

4. Click in the **Pop User Name** text box, then type your POP user ID.

Now you'll enter your personal information, which Netscape will use when you send, forward, or reply to e-mail messages.

5. Click the **Identity** tab in the Preferences dialog box to open personal identification text boxes. See Figure 3-3.

Figure 3-3 ◀
E-mail Identity
preferences

type your full name

type your full Internet
e-mail address

click to save
configurations

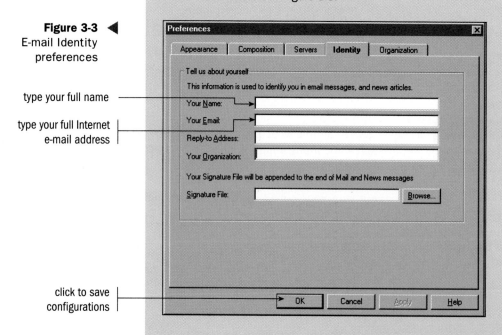

6. Click in the **Your Name** text box, then type your full name.

7. Press the **Tab** key to move to Your Email text box, then type your full e-mail address.

8. Press the **Tab** key to move to the Reply-to Address text box, then type your full e-mail address again.

9. Click the **OK** button to close the Preferences dialog box and configure Netscape for e-mail.

Now that you have configured Netscape for the e-mail function, you're ready to send e-mail messages.

Sending E-mail Messages

An e-mail message uses the same format as a standard memo: To, From, Date, Copies, Subject, and message. The Mail To line indicates who will receive the message. Netscape automatically fills in the From line with your name or e-mail address and the Date line with the current date when you send the message. The Cc line indicates who will receive a copy of the message. The Subject line, although optional, tells the recipients of the message the general topic it will cover. Finally, the message content area contains the text of your message.

Kevin wants to see a copy of the information you get from the New Perspectives on the Internet Using Netscape Navigator site. You'll send an e-mail message to yourself as a reminder to forward the information to Kevin.

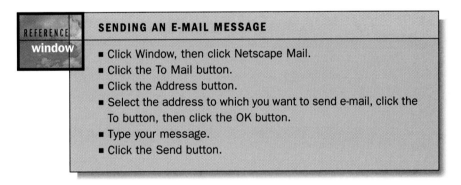

REFERENCE window

SENDING AN E-MAIL MESSAGE

- Click Window, then click Netscape Mail.
- Click the To Mail button.
- Click the Address button.
- Select the address to which you want to send e-mail, click the To button, then click the OK button.
- Type your message.
- Click the Send button.

To send an e-mail message:

1. Click **Window**, then click **Netscape Mail** to open the Mail window. See Figure 3-4.

Figure 3-4 ◀
Mail window

click to compose a
new e-mail message

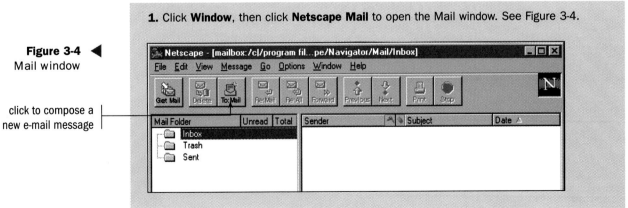

TROUBLE? If a message dialog box opens stating "No POP3 host has been specified in preferences," you need to tell Netscape the name of your host mail server. Click Options, click Mail and News Preferences, click Servers, then type the host server name provided by your technical support person in the Incoming mail server (POP) text box.

TROUBLE? If the Password Entry dialog box opens, Netscape might be set to automatically check for incoming e-mail when you open the Mail window. Type your POP password in the text box and then press the Enter key. If you don't know your POP password, ask your technical support person for help.

2. Click the **To Mail** button 📧 on the Mail toolbar to open the Message Composition window. See Figure 3-5.

Figure 3-5 ◀
Message
Composition
window

click to send mail ⟶

type recipient's e-mail
address here

type message here ⟶

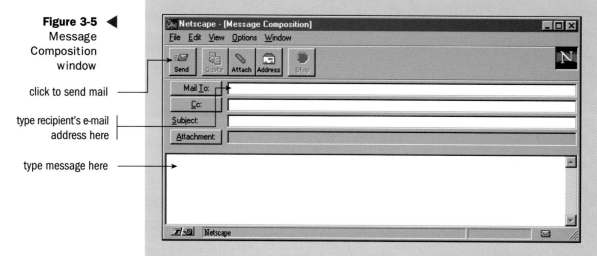

TROUBLE? If a message dialog opens indicating "Your email address has not been specified," you need to enter your e-mail information. Click Options, click Mail and News Preferences, click Identity, then enter your full e-mail address in the Your Email text box.

3. Click in the **Mail To** text box, and then type your full e-mail address.

4. Click in the **Subject** text box, and then type **Netscape E-mail Information**. Though not required, including a subject for your message will help you remember what it contains.

5. Click in the message content area, then type **Don't forget to send any information from the New Perspectives on the Internet Using Netscape Navigator site to Kevin.**

6. Click the **Send** button 📧 on the Mail Composition toolbar to send the e-mail message to yourself.

TROUBLE? If a message dialog box opens, indicating "A network error occurred: unable to connect to server," the server might be too busy to take your message. Click the Send button 📧 again. If you get the same message, you need to check the configuration of your host mail server. Click Options, click Mail and News Preferences, click Servers, and then type the server name provided by your technical support person in the Outgoing mail server (SMTP) text box.

E-MAIL NETIQUETTE

When you prepare an e-mail message, you should remember some commonsense guidelines.

- **Think before you type, read before you send.** Your name and your institution's name are attached to everything you send.
- **Type in both uppercase and lowercase letters.** Using all uppercase letters in e-mail messages is considered shouting, whereas messages in all lowercase letters are difficult to read and decipher.
- **Edit your message.** Keep your messages concise so the reader can understand your meaning quickly and clearly.
- **Send appropriate amounts of useful information.** Like junk mail, e-mail messages can pile up quickly.
- **Find out if personal e-mail messages are allowed on a work account.** E-mail is not free (businesses pay to subscribe to a server) nor is what you write and send from the workplace confidential.

With the message sent, you can create an Address Book, which lists the e-mail addresses for all the employees at Global Marketers.

Creating an Address Book

You need to address an e-mail message you want to send across the Net, just as you need to address a letter you want to send through the postal service. Like the wrong ZIP code on a letter, any misspelled words or incorrect punctuation in an e-mail address will result in an undeliverable message. Because memorizing many e-mail addresses is a cumbersome task, prone to errors, Netscape provides an Address Book in which you can record any number of e-mail addresses. For each address, Netscape stores a full name, a nickname, an e-mail address, and a description. Some businesses use the optional description category to include a company name or something else that further identifies the person. When you want to send an e-mail message to someone, you can just type that person's nickname or click the name from the Address Book list; Netscape will fill in the rest of the address information.

Global Marketers has one manager and several employees at each branch office. In order to test the system, you'll enter only the e-mail addressees for Kevin, Jane, and Megan, the three managers. Later, you can enter the e-mail addresses for the rest of the employees at Global Marketers. So you can use the same Address Book on different computers at various locations, you'll save the Address Book for Global Marketers to a disk. The Address Book for Global Marketers then will be separate from the Address Book stored on your computer.

ADDING AN ENTRY TO THE ADDRESS BOOK

- Click Window, then click Address book.
- In the Address Book window, click Item, then click Add User.
- Type the nickname in all lowercase letters, press the Tab key, type the full name, press the Tab key, type the e-mail address, press the Tab key, then type a description.
- Click the OK button.

To save an Address Book file to disk:

1. Click **Window**, then click **Address book** to open the Address Book window. See Figure 3-6.

name of Netscape's
address file

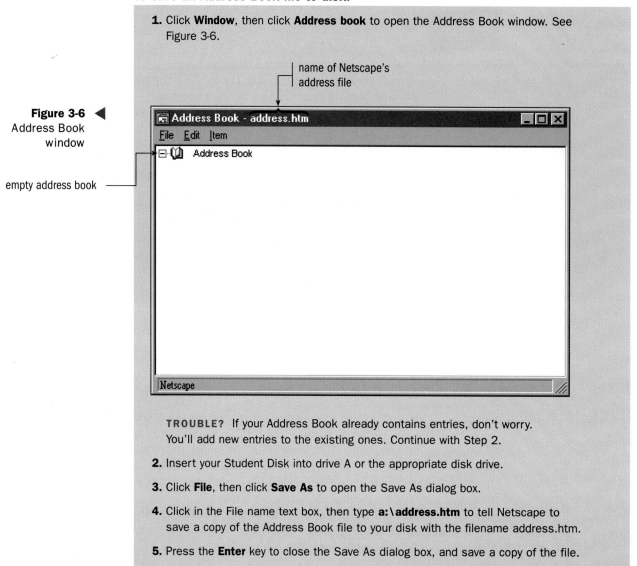

Figure 3-6
Address Book
window

empty address book

TROUBLE? If your Address Book already contains entries, don't worry. You'll add new entries to the existing ones. Continue with Step 2.

2. Insert your Student Disk into drive A or the appropriate disk drive.

3. Click **File**, then click **Save As** to open the Save As dialog box.

4. Click in the File name text box, then type **a:\address.htm** to tell Netscape to save a copy of the Address Book file to your disk with the filename address.htm.

5. Press the **Enter** key to close the Save As dialog box, and save a copy of the file.

With the Address Book file saved to your disk, you're ready to begin adding addresses for Kevin, Jane, and Megan.

To add an address:

1. In the Address Book window, click **Item**, then click **Add User** to open the Address Book dialog box.

   You'll enter the information for Kevin first.

2. Type **kevin** in the Nick Name text box using only lowercase letters and press the **Tab** key to move to the Name text box, type **Kevin Maki** and press the **Tab** key to move to the E-Mail Address text box, type **kmaki@ib.netcom.com** and press the **Tab** key to move to the Description text box, then type **Manager, U.S. branch**. The completed dialog box should match Figure 3-7.

Figure 3-7 ◀
Completed
Address Book
dialog box

type nicknames in
lowercase letters only

include both the user
ID and the host name

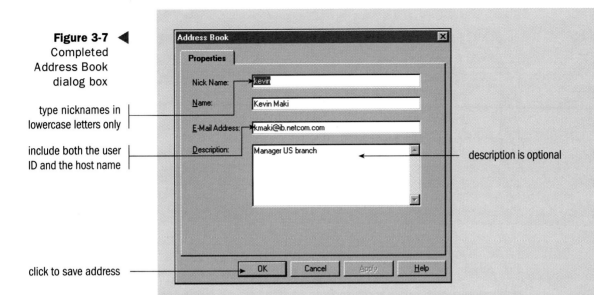

description is optional

click to save address

3. Click the **OK** button to save Kevin's information and close the Address Book dialog box. Notice that his name is preceded by a person icon, indicating that the
entry contains one person's address.

   TROUBLE? If a message dialog box opens with a message about the nickname,
   you might have typed the name with a capital letter. Click the OK button, click
   Kevin Maki to highlight the entry in the Address Book window. Then click Item,
   click Properties, type kevin in the Nick Name text box in all lowercase letters,
   then click the OK button.

   Now you'll enter the information for the manager of the office in England.

4. Repeat Steps 1 to 3 to enter the following information for Jane in the Address
   Book dialog box, pressing the **Tab** key to move to the next text box:

   jane
   Jane Phillips
   jphillips@ic.linkcom.uk
   Manager, England branch

   Notice that Netscape automatically reorders the entries in alphabetical order by
   the first letter of the entry in the Name text box.

5. Repeat Steps 1 to 3 to enter the following information for Megan, manager of
   the German office, in the Address Book dialog box, pressing the **Tab** key to move
   to the next text box:

   meg
   Megan Wolfe
   mwolfe@idx.interlink.de
   Manager, German branch

   You also need to create an Address Book entry for yourself so you can send
   e-mail to yourself to test a new address entry, read your e-mail messages from
   another location, or mail yourself a reminder.

6. Repeat Steps 1 to 3 to enter your own information. You can use any nickname
   for yourself. Your Address Book should look similar to Figure 3-8.

Figure 3-8 ◀
New Address
Book entries

icon represents a
person's address

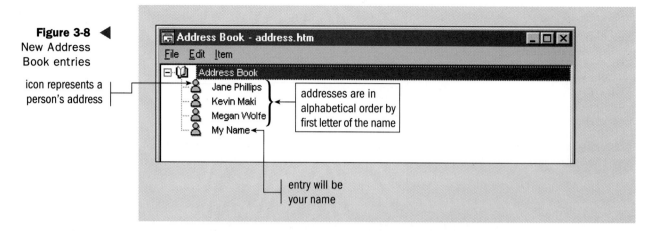

The Address Book list simplifies addressing an e-mail message. Sometimes you'll want to regularly send the same e-mail message to a group of people.

Grouping Address Book Entries

When you want to send multiple copies of an e-mail message to a group of people, you could manually select each name or type multiple nicknames every time, but this can be time-consuming and it's easy to miss someone. Rather than sending copies of the message individually, you can create a **list**, a specified group of Address Book entries, within the main Address Book. For example, Jane will want a group list that contains all the employees at the England office so she can easily send them policy messages or company reports. A list is identified by a nickname and a header label instead of a name, but it does not have an e-mail address. For example, Jane might name the list England Office Employees. Every person in the list has an e-mail address, but the group as a whole does not. You can copy each entry in the main Address Book into as many lists as you need; Netscape adds that name to the list as an **alias**, which is a shortcut telling Netscape where to find the necessary e-mail information.

At Global Marketers, Kevin, Megan, and Jane each want a group list that contains their e-mail addresses so they can quickly exchange information about company finances, planning strategies, meetings, and so forth. Kevin asks you to create a list for the three branch managers.

To create a list:

1. Click **Item**, then click **Add List** to open the Address Book dialog box again.

2. Enter the following information in the dialog box (remember to press the **Tab** key to move to the next text box): type **managers** in the Nick Name text box, type **Top Management** in the Name text box, then type **Global Marketers branch management** in the Description text box.

3. Click the **OK** button to create the new list, and close the Address Book dialog box. See Figure 3-9.

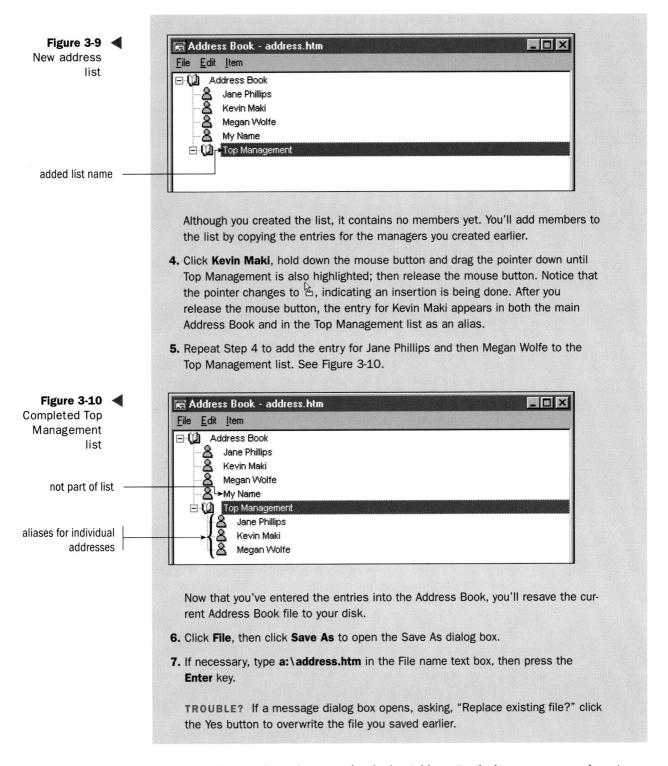

Figure 3-9 ◀
New address
list

added list name ——

Although you created the list, it contains no members yet. You'll add members to the list by copying the entries for the managers you created earlier.

4. Click **Kevin Maki**, hold down the mouse button and drag the pointer down until Top Management is also highlighted; then release the mouse button. Notice that the pointer changes to 🖑, indicating an insertion is being done. After you release the mouse button, the entry for Kevin Maki appears in both the main Address Book and in the Top Management list as an alias.

5. Repeat Step 4 to add the entry for Jane Phillips and then Megan Wolfe to the Top Management list. See Figure 3-10.

Figure 3-10 ◀
Completed Top
Management
list

not part of list ——

aliases for individual
addresses

Now that you've entered the entries into the Address Book, you'll resave the current Address Book file to your disk.

6. Click **File**, then click **Save As** to open the Save As dialog box.

7. If necessary, type **a:\address.htm** in the File name text box, then press the **Enter** key.

TROUBLE? If a message dialog box opens, asking, "Replace existing file?" click the Yes button to overwrite the file you saved earlier.

Kevin tells you that when you finish the Address Book, he wants to send copies to Megan and Jane so they can add the entries for the U.S. office to their Address Books.

Importing an Address File

Importing a file merges the information from one file into another. For example, when Megan imports Kevin's Address Book file, the information from Kevin's file will be incorporated or added into her Address Book. Netscape opens a message dialog box whenever an imported entry is the same as an existing entry or an imported list is the same as an existing list. Netscape adds the imported data, creating duplicate entries and lists in the Address Book.

You want to make sure that Megan and Jane will be able to import the Address Book without any problems before you send it to them. You'll test Netscape's importing capabilities with the file you just saved.

To import an address file:

1. Click **File**, then click **Import** to open the Import dialog box.

2. Double-click **address.htm** from the list of files. A message dialog box opens, indicating that the imported entry is the same as an entry in the Address Book. This same dialog box will reopen for each duplicated entry or list—five in all. See Figure 3-11.

Figure 3-11 ◀
Duplication
warning

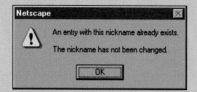

TROUBLE? If you don't see the address file you just saved in the file list, type a:\address.htm in the File name text box, and press the Enter key.

3. Click the **OK** button five times to close every message dialog box.

   The Address Book on your hard disk now contains a duplicate of each entry, verifying that your saved file contains the correct information.

4. Click **File**, then click **Close** to close the Address Book window.

When the branch offices of Global Marketers import the file into their Address Book, they'll be able to exchange e-mail messages easily. You'll use the address file to send an e-mail message that contains the Address Book file to all three managers.

Using the Address Book

Using the Address Book is even easier than creating it. Whenever you want to send an e-mail message to a person or a group of people, you can select any combination or number of personal entries and list entries from the Address Book.

To test Netscape's Address Book and the e-mail function, you'll send a message to the Top Management list, the three managers of Global Marketers.

To use the Address Book to address an e-mail message:

1. Click the **To Mail** button 🖾 on the toolbar to open the Message Composition window.

2. Click the **Address** button 🖾 on the Message Composition toolbar to open the Select Addresses dialog box. See Figure 3-12.

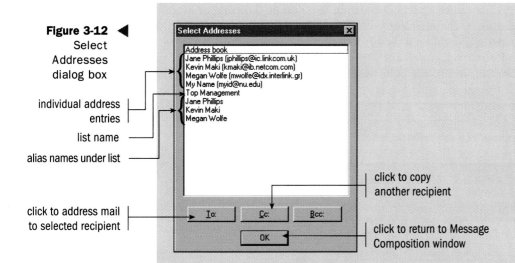

Figure 3-12 ◄
Select
Addresses
dialog box

individual address
entries

list name

alias names under list

click to copy
another recipient

click to address mail
to selected recipient

click to return to Message
Composition window

You could select the name of each person you want to send the e-mail message to, but it's easier just to select the list of managers you created earlier.

3. Click **Top Management** from the list of addresses, then click the **To** button. Kevin, Jane, and Megan will each receive the e-mail message because Netscape automatically includes the e-mail addresses for everyone on that list.

   You decide to send a copy of the message to yourself so you can be certain that the message was sent correctly.

4. Click your name from the list of addresses, then click the **Cc** button. ("Cc" is an abbreviation for carbon copy, a holdover from the days of typewriters, that simply means you're sending a courtesy copy to that person.)

5. Click the **OK** button to close the Select Addresses dialog box. Notice that Netscape inserts the address names into the Mail To and Cc text boxes.

6. Type **Test message** in the Subject text box. Though not required, including a subject helps the recipient anticipate the e-mail message.

   Kevin suggests that you send Megan and Jane the address file with the e-mail message. You'll let them know that they should look for the file in your message.

7. Type **This is a test message with a file attached**. in the message content area.

Kevin wants you to attach the Address Book to the e-mail you just wrote, so you won't send the e-mail message yet. Attaching a file to an e-mail message is a convenient and speedy way to transfer a file from one person to another.

Attaching a File to an E-mail Message

When two people work in the same office or use the same local area network (LAN), it is relatively easy to share files because they share a common server and can open each other's files. When people work in different states or even different countries, however, they need to mail disks to each other, which can be expensive and take a day or longer to receive. Attaching a file to an e-mail message is an easy and effective way to send files as long as both people use the same or compatible e-mail programs. The recipient receives the attached file just as quickly as any other electronic message.

A file can be attached to e-mail in its original format or as a plain text file with no formatting. If the recipient will open the file with the same program you used to create it, then you should send the file in its original format. This ensures that the document retains its formatting as well as its text. For example, if you create an Excel spreadsheet and send the resulting .xls file in its original format, the recipient will receive an .xls file that retains the formatting and calculation codes and can open the file in Excel. If you know that the person you want to send the file to doesn't have Excel (or the program you used to create the file), you can send it as plain text, which strips a file of all its formatting and other coding, leaving only the text content.

REFERENCE
window

ATTACHING A FILE TO AN E-MAIL MESSAGE

- In the Message Composition window, click View, then click Attachments as Links.
- Click the Attach button.
- In the Attachments dialog box, click the Attach File button.
- Enter or select the filename of the file you want to attach, then press the Enter key.
- Click the OK button.

To attach a file to an e-mail message:

1. In the Message Composition window, click **View**, then click **Attachments as Links** so that any files you attach to your e-mail message will be saved separately, rather than incorporated into the text of the e-mail message.

2. Click the **Attach** button to open the Attachments dialog box.

3. Click the **Attach File** button to open the Enter file to attach dialog box.

4. Click in the File name text box, type **a:\address.htm** to tell Netscape to attach the address file located on your disk, then press the **Enter** key. The Enter file to attach dialog box closes, and the address file is listed in the Attachments dialog box. See Figure 3-13.

Figure 3-13 ◀
Attachments
dialog box

file to attach ——

click to retain native
format

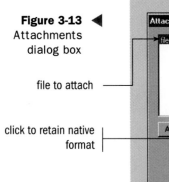
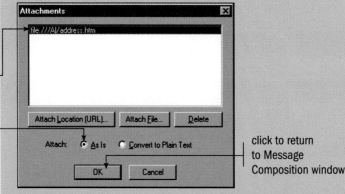

click to return
to Message
Composition window

The As Is radio button is the default, indicating that the file will be sent in whatever format it was created. In this case, the address file is an HTML Web document and will be sent as an .htm file that any installation of Netscape can read.

5. Click the **OK** button to close the Attachments dialog box and return to the Message Composition window. See Figure 3-14.

Figure 3-14 ◀
Completed
Message
Composition
window

click to send mail ───

recipient address ───

attached file ───

message
content area ───

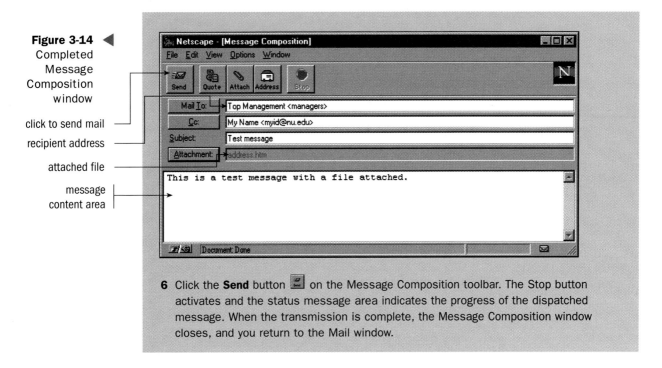

6 Click the **Send** button 🖂 on the Message Composition toolbar. The Stop button activates and the status message area indicates the progress of the dispatched message. When the transmission is complete, the Message Composition window closes, and you return to the Mail window.

Now that you've sent the e-mail message with an attached file to Kevin, Jane, Megan, and yourself, you want to check to see if you received the e-mail message.

Receiving E-mail Messages

Recall that e-mail messages people send you are handled by a POP server. The POP server, similar to a post office, collects all mail associated with a given region (host) and holds it for pickup and delivery by a mail carrier (e-mail program). Acting as your mail carrier, Netscape contacts the POP server, requests any mail addressed to your user ID, and delivers it to your computer mailbox.

Rather than being limited to a fixed delivery schedule, you can check your e-mail at any time. When you ask Netscape to check for incoming mail, it sends a request to the POP server, which returns only e-mail messages that arrived since you last checked. Some people check for new e-mail messages sporadically during the day, while others check at regular intervals, such as every hour or every morning and night.

The e-mail messages can be stored on the POP server or in your own computer's memory. When e-mail is left on the server, you can access it from any computer with an e-mail program, whether at school, home, or work. However, once you move the e-mail to a specific computer, you can access it only from that computer. Storing many e-mail messages on a computer can consume a lot of disk space. To conserve space, many network administrators don't allow people to store e-mail messages on the server after they have been read.

You sent a test message to the top managers at Global Marketers with a copy to yourself. You want to make sure the messages were delivered successfully.

To check for incoming mail:

1. Click the **Get Mail** 🖳 button on the Mail toolbar to accept all incoming mail since the last time you checked. You will be asked for your password, personal code that verifies you have the right to read the incoming mail.

2. Type your password into the Password Entry dialog box, then click the **OK** button to receive your mail. The status message area indicates the number of messages you are receiving and which message is currently loading. When all incoming messages are received, the status message area reads "Document: Done."

TROUBLE? If you don't know your password, ask your instructor or technical support person for help.

TROUBLE? If a message dialog box opens, indicating "The POP3 server does not support the UIDL command. Without support of this we cannot implement the 'keep mail on server' and 'maximum message size' preferences. These options have been disabled and messages will be removed from the server after being downloaded." then you cannot store messages you have already read on the server. Click the OK button, then continue with the tutorial.

TROUBLE? If a message dialog box opens, indicating "Netscape is unable to use the POP3 server because you have not provided a username." you need to tell Netscape your user ID so it can check for your mail. Click Options, click Mail and News Preferences, click Servers, type your user ID in the Pop User Name text box, then click the OK button.

You should have received at least four new messages since you last checked your e-mail messages, including the reminder message you sent yourself, the test message you sent yourself, and the e-mail message you requested earlier.

Reading and Replying to E-mail Messages

You can open, read, and reply to e-mail messages from the Mail window, the same window you told Netscape to check for new messages. Netscape's Mail window is split into three panes, or parts. The **Mail Folder pane** in the upper-left corner shows the folders used to organize your mail: the Inbox folder contains all the e-mail messages you receive, the Sent folder contains copies of all the e-mail messages you send, and the Trash folder contains all the e-mail messages you discard. The **Sender pane** in the upper-right corner shows the contents of each folder in the left pane when you click it. For example, when you select the Inbox folder, you'll see the individual incoming e-mail messages: both new messages you received since the last time you checked your e-mail and old messages you haven't yet discarded. When an e-mail message subject is too long to fit in the Subject column, you see the beginning of the subject followed by an ellipsis (...). When you select an e-mail message in the Sender pane, the contents of that message are displayed in the **Message pane** below it. You can resize all three panes by clicking the edge of the pane and dragging in the appropriate direction. For example, to enlarge the Message pane so you can see more of a message at once, click the top edge of the pane and drag it toward the top of the window until the pane is the size you want.

Often, you'll want to respond to questions or comments included in an e-mail message. When you reply to an e-mail message, you respond to the original sender of the message.

You'll read the e-mail message you received since you last checked your Inbox folder.

To read and reply to an e-mail message:

1. Click the **Inbox** folder in the Mail Folder pane to show all incoming messages. See Figure 3-15. Your Inbox folder might contain additional e-mail messages.

Figure 3-15
Incoming
messages

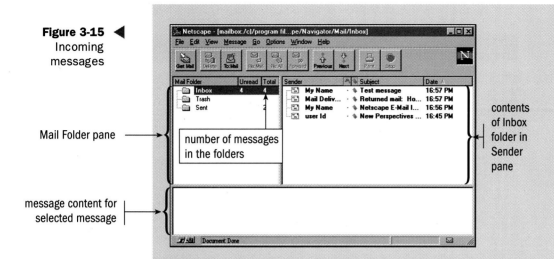

Mail Folder pane

number of messages
in the folders

message content for
selected message

contents
of Inbox
folder in
Sender
pane

Recall that earlier you sent yourself a reminder message. You'll look at that message first.

2. Click **Netscape E-mail Information** in the Subject column of the Sender pane. The message opens into the Message pane.

3. If necessary, enlarge the viewing area by clicking the top of the pane and dragging up, release the mouse button when the pane is the size you want. Scroll through the Message pane to read the message.

You realize that you should send a copy of the same information to Megan and Jane, but you first want to verify that they were able to read your earlier message. You could just send yourself another e-mail message, but it's easier to reply to the one that's already open.

4. Click the **Re Mail** button [image] on the Mail toolbar to open the Reply window. See Figure 3-16.

Figure 3-16
Reply window

your e-mail
address name will
appear here

Netscape adds
automatically

type new message
above original

The Reply window works just like the Message Composition window does, except that Netscape already fills in the Mail To text box and the Subject text box.

5. Click in the message content area and type **Don't forget to send this same information to Megan and Jane too.** to add this message above your earlier one.

TROUBLE? If the original message doesn't appear in the message content area, click the Quote button on the Reply toolbar, then repeat Step 5.

6. Click the **Send** button [image] on the Reply toolbar to send the message to yourself.

Now that you've responded to that e-mail message, you'll read another one.

Saving and Reading Attachments

When you receive an e-mail message with an attached file in a format Netscape does not recognize, you must save the file and open it with the correct program. Clicking the attachment is similar to clicking a hypertext link. If Netscape recognizes the file extension of the attachment as belonging to a program on its Helper list it will open the file. If it does not recognize the file extension, then you need to tell Netscape to save the file.

To save an attached file:

1. Click **New Perspectives on the Internet Using Netscape Navigator** in the Subject column to open that message into the Message pane.

   TROUBLE? If you don't see the entire subject shown in Step 1, but do see the first words of the message, then the Subject column is too small to see the entire Subject. Click the abbreviated subject and continue with Step 2.

2. Read the e-mail message. When you reach the end of the message, you see an attachment box, indicating that a file is attached to this e-mail. See Figure 3-17.

Figure 3-17 ◀
Attachment
box

click to save file
attachment

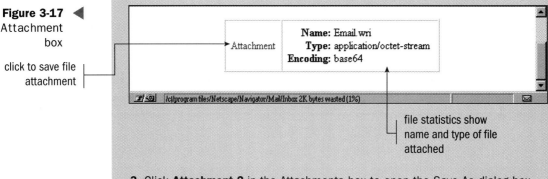

file statistics show
name and type of file
attached

3. Click **Attachment 2** in the Attachments box to open the Save As dialog box.

4. Type **a:\email.wri** in the File name text box, make sure your Student Disk is in drive A or the appropriate disk drive, then press the **Enter** key to save the attached file to your disk.

5. After you exit Netscape, open this file in a word-processing program such as Windows NotePad or WordPad, to see the fully formatted file.

Now look at the copy of the test message you sent to yourself. It also has a file attached, but one that Netscape recognizes—HTML. When Netscape recognizes the filename extension, you can have it open the file within the text of the message, or **inline**. Because this attached file is an HTML file, Netscape also can display the file as a Web page.

To view an attachment inline:

1. Click **View**, then click **Attachments Inline**. Netscape will open and display any attachments within the message when it recognizes the filename extension.

2. Click **Test message** in the Subject column to display the message contents in the Message pane.

3. Scroll down to read the message. Notice that the attached address file is open and displayed inline. See Figure 3-18.

Figure 3-18 ◀
File attachment
inline

contents of the file
displayed inline with
message

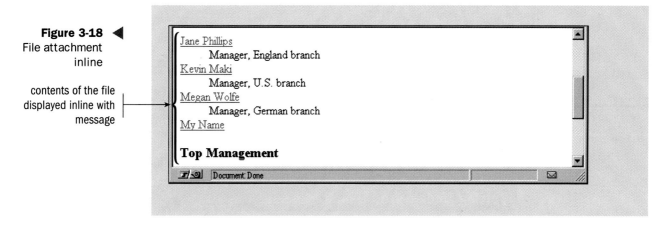

Now that you have sent, received, and opened e-mail messages with Netscape, you want to try out the e-mail program's forwarding capabilities.

Forwarding Mail

Forwarding is similar to replying to an e-mail message, except that when you forward an e-mail message, you send a copy of the entire message to another person. When you click the Forward button on the Mail toolbar, Netscape fills in the Subject text box, and, if applicable, the Attachment text box, with information from the original message. The Mail To text box remains blank so you can fill in a new recipient from the Address Book. When forwarding a message, you can add new comments to the original text of the message in the outgoing message area.

Global Marketers will use this feature frequently in its international communications. You'll forward a copy of this e-mail message now to see how well it works.

To forward mail:

1. Click **Test message** in the Subject column to select the message.

2. Click the **Forward** button 🔲 on the Mail toolbar to forward this message. The partially completed Message Composition window opens. The Subject text box includes the original subject title preceded by "Fwd" to show the recipient that this is a forwarded mailing. The Attachment text box references the file attached to the original message. See Figure 3-19.

Figure 3-19 ◀
Forward
window

indicates a forwarded
message rather than
an original mailing

original mail is
attached to this
message

any message content
entered here will be
added to the front of
the original message
content

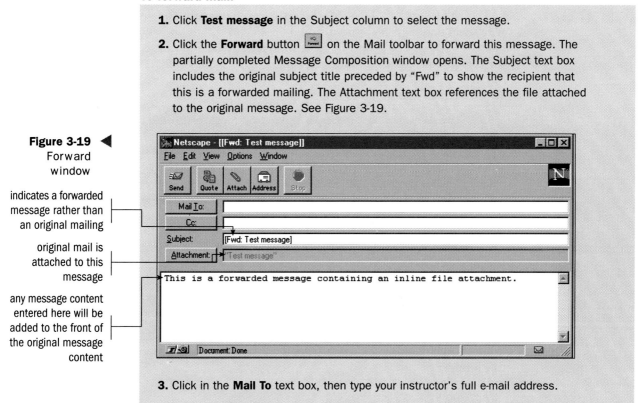

3. Click in the **Mail To** text box, then type your instructor's full e-mail address.

> **4.** Press the **Tab** key to move to the Cc text box, and then type your full e-mail address.
>
> **5.** Click in the message content area, then type **This is a forwarded message containing an inline file attachment.** to add new text before the forwarded message.
>
> **6.** Click the **Send** button on the Forward toolbar to dispatch the message.

You still have another message in the Inbox folder that you haven't viewed.

Getting Undelivered E-mail Messages

Sometimes you send an e-mail message to an Internet address that is no longer active, such as when a person changes his or her e-mail service to another server or switches to a different online service provider. When the SMTP server, which handles your outgoing mail, cannot locate an e-mail address that matches the recipient's address in the Mail To text box, you will receive an undeliverable mail message, like the ones you have for the test messages you sent to Kevin, Megan, and Jane. This is similar to the postal service returning a letter because the street address is incorrect.

If e-mail messages you send are returned undelivered, you should verify the e-mail addresses that you used. Make sure that everything is typed correctly and the person is still using that e-mail address.

You decide to keep a copy of the test message and try sending it again after you verify with Kevin the addresses you have for Kevin, Megan, and Jane.

Saving and Deleting E-Mail Messages

As you receive e-mail messages, you'll want to save messages that you want to keep and continually delete those you no longer need so the Inbox folder doesn't become cluttered.

The employees at Global Marketers travel frequently and sometimes take messages with them that they might need stored on disk. A disk is an easy way to transport saved e-mail messages. You'll save the Test Message so that you can send it again after you get the correct e-mail addresses for everyone.

To save e-mail messages to a disk:

> **1.** If necessary, click **Test message** in the Subject column to select it.
>
> **2.** Click **File**, then click **Save As** to open the Save As dialog box.
>
> **3.** If necessary, highlight the text in the File name text box, then type **a:\testmsg.txt** to name the file your saving to your disk. Netscape uses the default filename "Inbox" for saved messages, but you can save only one file with that name. Instead, you should use a name that indicates the content of the message. In this case, you used testmsg, an abbreviation of the Subject text box (test message).
>
> **4.** Make sure your Student Disk is in drive A or the appropriate disk drive, then press the **Enter** key to save the file to your disk.

After you have read a message and replied to or forwarded it as necessary, you can delete it. Any message you delete from the Inbox folder is transferred automatically to the Trash folder.

To delete an e-mail message:

1. If necessary, click **Test message** in the Subject column to select it.

2. Click the **Delete** button ⬛ on the Mail toolbar to move the message to the Trash folder. Notice that the number in the Inbox Total column of the Mail Folder pane decreased by one and the number in the Trash folder increased by one.

3. Repeat Steps 1 and 2 to remove any other messages you want to delete.

   Deleted messages remain in the Trash folder, providing an opportunity to retrieve them, until you empty the Trash folder. To completely remove e-mail messages and free up storage space available in your computer's memory, you must empty the Trash folder.

4. Click **File**, then click **Empty Trash Folder** to remove the contents of the Trash folder. The status message area shows the process of deleting the contents of the Trash folder. Notice that the number in the Trash Total column is now zero.

   Netscape automatically compacts the folders to a size just large enough to hold the remaining mail to recover the storage space made available by emptying the Trash folder.

Just as you want to keep your Inbox clean and up-to-date, you'll want to make sure that the Address Book contains only relevant entries.

Deleting Address Book Entries

Periodically, you'll want to remove outdated or no-longer-needed entries from your Address Book. For example, you no longer need an entry for an employee who leaves Global Marketers. Because you saved the addresses for Global Marketers to your disk, you can delete them from the Address Book on your computer.

To delete entries from the Address Book:

1. Click **Window**, then click **Address book** to open the Address Book window.

2. Click the first **Top Management** list to highlight it.

3. Click **Edit**, then **Delete** to remove the list.

4. Click the first **Jane Phillips** entry to highlight it.

5. Click **Edit**, then click **Delete**. A message dialog box opens indicating that Jane is also part of a list as an alias. If you delete the entry for Jane, Netscape will remove her alias from any list that includes her name.

   TROUBLE? If the message dialog does not open, you already deleted all the lists that included Jane's alias and Netscape removes the entry. Skip Step 6.

6. Click the **OK** button to close the dialog box and delete the entry for Jane.

Although you could delete each item one at a time, it is faster to delete them all at once. Just press and hold down the Ctrl key while you select the entries you want to delete. You'll do this for the rest of the Address Book entries for Global Marketers.

To delete a group of entries:

1. Click **Jane Phillips**, the top address entry of the Address Book for Global Marketers.

2. Press and hold the **Ctrl** key while you click to select the remaining entries for Global Marketers, including both entries for Kevin Maki and Megan Wolfe, and the entry for Top Management.

3. Release the **Ctrl** key. All the remaining entries for Global Marketers are highlighted. See Figure 3-20.

Figure 3-20 ◄
Deleting
highlighted
entries

select these entries ──────

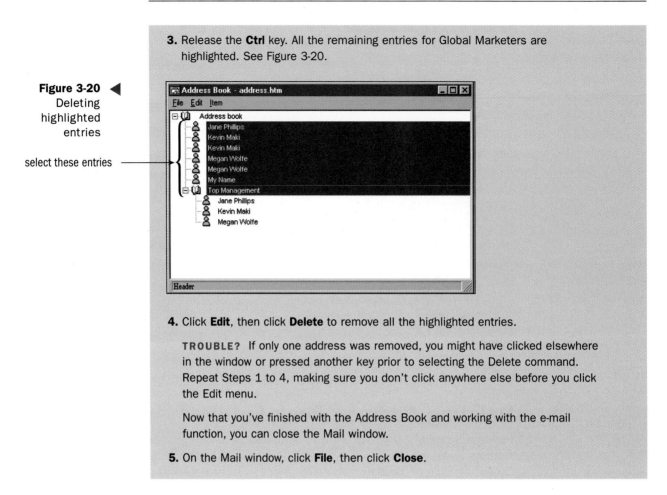

4. Click **Edit**, then click **Delete** to remove all the highlighted entries.

TROUBLE? If only one address was removed, you might have clicked elsewhere in the window or pressed another key prior to selecting the Delete command. Repeat Steps 1 to 4, making sure you don't click anywhere else before you click the Edit menu.

Now that you've finished with the Address Book and working with the e-mail function, you can close the Mail window.

5. On the Mail window, click **File**, then click **Close**.

The e-mail functions in Netscape work well and will help contribute to the success of Global Marketers. Kevin asks you to work on transferring files between the offices while he verifies the e-mail addresses for Jane and Megan.

Quick Check

1 In the e-mail address jdoe@mu.edu, "jdoe" is the _____ and "mu.edu" is the _____.

2 You can store e-mail addresses in the _____ .

3 True or False: You can view and read an attachment to an e-mail message, but you cannot save it.

4 When you want to send a copy of an e-mail message to someone, you enter that person's e-mail address in the _____ text box.

5 Before Netscape will check if you have any new e-mail addresses, you must enter a valid _____.

6 What happens to e-mail messages that have incorrect or obsolete e-mail addresses?

7 True or False: You can store e-mail messages you receive only on the host server.

8 True or False: Clicking the Delete button when an Inbox message is highlighted will permanently remove the e-mail message from disk storage.

You have completed Session 3.1. If you aren't going to work through Session 3.2 now, you should exit Netscape. When you are ready to begin Session 3.2, launch Netscape, make sure the toolbar, directory buttons, and location box are visible and images are set to auto load, and then continue with the session.

SESSION

3.2

In this session, you will download programs stored on other computers, check them for viruses, uncompress files, and use shareware programs.

Transferring Files

Kevin asks you to focus on obtaining and setting up programs that the office should have. For example, because Global Marketers will send files of word-processing documents and HTML files of proposed Web pages between its clients and three offices, Kevin wants a program that compresses (shrinks) files (and thus are quicker to transfer between computers) and then expands them again. After you have this one program, he wants you to look for other types of programs that might be useful for the office.

In order to get files from a server on the Internet to your computer, you need to use File Transfer Protocol (FTP). **FTP** provides a means of logging onto, or connecting to, a computer elsewhere on the Internet (called a **remote computer**), viewing its directories, and transferring files to and from your local computer. Recall that a protocol is the standard, or set of rules, by which computers communicate. FTP is the protocol whose function is to efficiently transfer files. You can quickly recognize an FTP site by its URL, which begins with "ftp://" instead of "http://" or "gopher://."

The person who owns or runs each server can decide whether to establish a **public directory**, a portion of the server that stores files that people inside, and sometimes outside, that company or organization can upload or download. **Upload** means to transfer a copy of a file from your own computer to a public directory. **Download** means to transfer a copy of a file from the public directory to your own computer.

When you upload or download files to and from a remote server, you usually need a **log-on ID** and **password**, codes that identify the person connecting to the server and control access to network files. If access to the server is restricted, you'll need the proper log-on ID and password. When a server is open to anyone on the Internet, usually the log-on ID is "anonymous" and the password is "guest" or your full e-mail address. These sites are referred to as **anonymous FTP sites**. Administrators of anonymous FTP sites often allow anyone to download files from their servers, but don't allow people to upload to the servers, so they can control what files are added to their servers. When you connect to an anonymous FTP site, Netscape automatically supplies the log-on ID and password needed to access the remote computer.

USES AND abuses

ANONYMOUS FTP

The ability to upload and download files to and from any public directory in the world is one way the Internet is shrinking traditional global boundaries. Anonymous FTP:

- Permits efficient, worldwide sharing of files between computers.
- Creates an inexpensive means of distributing programs for authors.
- Provides easy access to try-before-you-buy shareware.
- Unfortunately, also spreads viruses due to unrestricted public access.

Kevin mentioned that Global Marketers will need to transfer files frequently between the three offices, to and from clients, and to and from the Internet using FTP and e-mail attachments. Such files might be large because they contain graphics and take a long time to transfer, so any files sent to and from Global Marketers will be compressed. The first program Kevin wants you to locate is an uncompression program.

Downloading an Uncompression Program

The length of time a file takes to transfer over the Internet depends largely on the speed of the computer modem and on the size of the file. In order to conserve space on a network server and decrease the time a file takes to transfer, many files are compressed. **Compression** compacts data into a smaller size by scanning a file, eliminating duplicate words or phrases, and replacing them with reference codes, which it keeps in a small internal chart that accompanies the compressed file. For example, the word "Netscape" might be replaced by a code such as "#1" every time it appears in these tutorials, decreasing the space it takes up by six characters. Apply this same coding to every repeated word in a lengthy document and its file can compress to a much smaller size. Often, several related files are compiled into a single compressed file. One popular compression program, pkzip, creates compressed files that appear with the extension .zip.

Before you can use a compressed file, you must **uncompress**, or expand, it to its original structure and size. An **uncompression utility** is a general-purpose program that explodes the compressed file into all its original component files. Figure 3-21 illustrates the file compression, transfer, and uncompression process.

Figure 3-21 ◀
File compression, transfer, and uncompression

2. compressed file is uploaded to the FTP server

1. remote computer compresses filea.exe into filea.zip

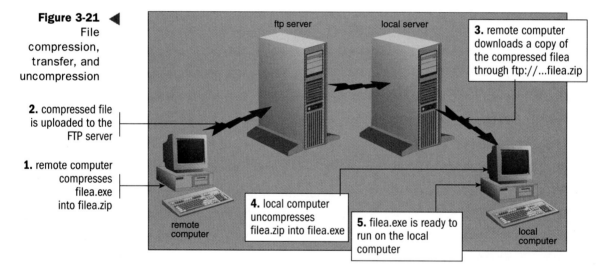

To enable Global Marketers employees to use compressed files that they download from the Internet, you need to locate an uncompression utility on an FTP site and download it to your computer. Kevin decided that he wants to use pkunzip, a popular and reliable program that is part of a group of programs stored in pkz204g.exe. When several programs are packed together, you download the entire group and select the programs you want to use later.

How are you going to find a copy of this file? Thousands of files are available from numerous FTP sites. Searching for the keywords "pkunzip download" with a Web search engine will likely turn up several FTP site referrals, but you'll have to sift through the many other references produced by the search query in order to find them. Recall that a Web search query checks the content of an Internet file as well as its URL, so you'll end up with many more references to check. Using an Archie service is a more direct method to locate a specific file.

Searching with Archie

Before the WWW existed, people relied on **Archie**, a system to locate files and information stored at anonymous FTP sites by filenames. Unlike Web search engines that reference content, Archie servers index only the filenames contained in a database. Although every Archie query form might look a bit different, they all work similarly. You enter a keyword query using the filename you want to find and click a button to start the search. In a few moments, you'll get a response. The resulting list of references includes only those FTP sites that have a copy of the program you want.

If you don't find the file you're looking for through one Archie, try a different one. Just as each Web spider updates its database on a different schedule, so do Archie servers. An Archie typically updates its database weekly and checks only selected FTP sites. Files that were added to that FTP site since the last update are not included in the query result.

To help you, Kevin collected a list of Archie servers and placed their links on a Web page. You'll begin by opening this Web page.

To open the Global Marketers, Inc. page:

1. Click **Options**, then click **Show Directory Buttons** to toggle off this option. Removing the directory buttons from view will leave more space on screen to view Web pages.

2. Click in the **Location** box to highlight the current URL.

3. Type **http://www.vmedia.com/cti/NewPerspectives/tiun** and then press the **Enter** key.

   TROUBLE? If a message dialog box opens indicating Netscape was unable to locate the server or cannot find the requested URL, you might have typed a character incorrectly. Click the OK button to close the dialog box, click the Location text box, use the arrow keys to move to any error, correct the character, then press the Enter key.

4. Click the **Tutorial 3** link, then click the **Global Marketers, Inc.** link to open the company's Web page. See Figure 3-22.

Figure 3-22 ◄
Global
Marketers, Inc.
page

list of Archie servers ──────

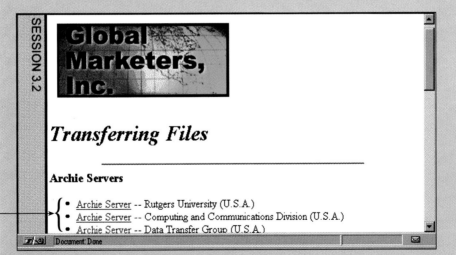

5. If necessary, scroll down the Web page until you see the section labeled "Archie Servers."

   Kevin grouped some Archie servers in this section that you can use to find the uncompression program he wants. You can use any of them to locate a site.

6. Click any Archie server link to open to a query form. The query form should look similar to Figure 3-23.

Figure 3-23 ◄
Archie query
form

Query text box ⎯⎯⎯⎯⎯

click to begin search ⎯⎯⎯⎯

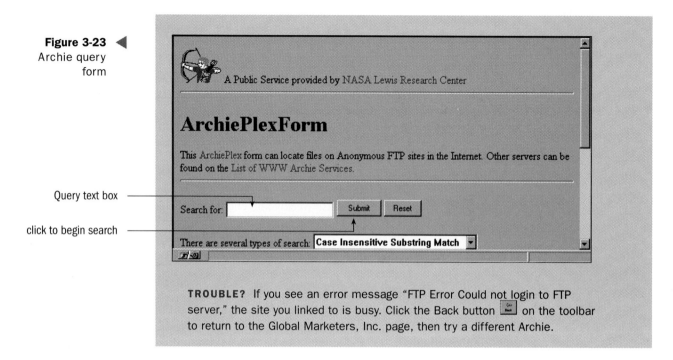

A Public Service provided by NASA Lewis Research Center

ArchiePlexForm

This ArchiePlex form can locate files on Anonymous FTP sites in the Internet. Other servers can be found on the List of WWW Archie Services.

Search for: [   ]   [Submit]   [Reset]

There are several types of search: [Case Insensitive Substring Match ▼]

TROUBLE? If you see an error message "FTP Error Could not login to FTP server," the site you linked to is busy. Click the Back button 🔲 on the toolbar to return to the Global Marketers, Inc. page, then try a different Archie.

Recall that the uncompression program you're looking for is called pkz204g.exe. Although this filename, pkz204g.exe, might seem cryptic, it is actually quite descriptive. Windows 95 permits long filenames, but DOS (Disk Operating System) and earlier versions of Windows restrict filenames to a maximum of eight characters with a filename extension of three characters. **DOS** is a type of operating system program. For Internet use, only these shorter filenames are used. In this case, "pkz" is an abbreviation for "pkzip"—the name of the program, "204g" indicates the version of the program, and the filename extension ".exe" indicates the file contains an executable program. So, fully decoded, the filename means that this file contains an executable copy of pkzip, version 2.04g.

You'll use Archie to locate a copy of pkz204g.exe.

To do an Archie search:

1. If necessary, scroll down until you see the query text box. Each Archie server query form is arranged somewhat differently, so you might have to scroll past several other text boxes. You don't need to change the entries in these text boxes.

2. Type **pkz204g.exe** in the Query text box to indicate the name of the program you want to find.

3. Click the **Submit**, **Start Search**, or **Send Request** button, or press the **Enter** key to begin the search. The name of the button depends on the Archie you're using. In a few moments, when the search is complete, you'll see a list of sites at which pkz204g.exe is available. See Figure 3-24.

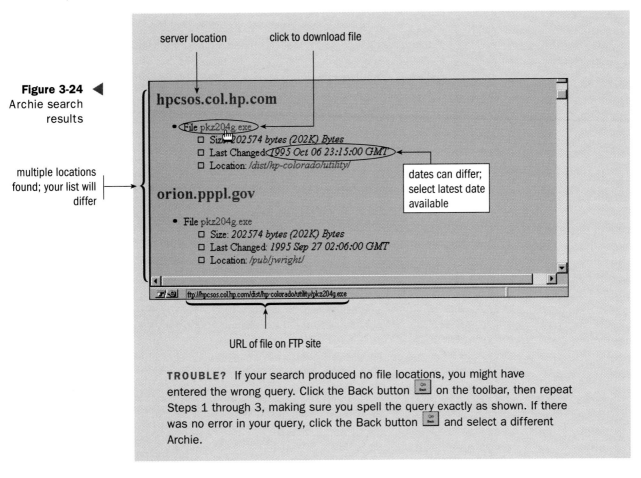

Figure 3-24 ◀
Archie search
results

multiple locations
found; your list will
differ

The list contains one or more FTP sites that contain the pkz204g.exe file. Now that you know where to find the file, you can download a copy.

Downloading an Uncompression Utility

An Archie search often produces more than one FTP site from which you can download the program or file you requested. (Recall that downloading means to transfer a copy of a file from a remote computer to your own.) The list of sites also includes dates of when the file was placed at that site. You should always scroll through the list and use the file with the most current date. Software that you download is frequently updated by the original developer or someone who wants to improve it. Though the file may have the same name, there can be slight changes to the accompanying files or the actual program. By selecting the most recent date, you are more likely to include the latest updates.

Now that you've found the uncompression utility that Kevin wants to use, you need to copy it from the remote computer to the one at Global Marketers.

To download a program:

1. Insert your Student Disk into drive A or the appropriate drive on your computer. Make sure you use the Student Disk for Session 3.2.

2. Create a folder named **pkzip** on your disk to help you keep the files you download organized. Click the right mouse button on the **Start** button in the Windows 95 taskbar, then click **Explore** to open the Windows Explorer program. Scroll up the All Folders panel, then click **3½ Floppy (A:)**, click **File**, position the pointer over **New**, click **Folder**, type **pkzip** as the folder name, press the **Enter** key, then click the **Close** button ☒ in the upper-right corner of the Explorer window.

TROUBLE? If the Windows 95 taskbar isn't visible, click the Minimize button ▬ in the upper-right corner of the Netscape window, then continue with Step 3.

TROUBLE? If you are using an earlier version of Windows, press and hold the Alt key while you press the Tab key until you see Program Manager, then release both keys. Locate and double-click the File Manager icon, click the A: button, click File, click Create Directory, type pkzip as the directory name, press the Enter key, click File, then click Exit. If Netscape is not in view, press and hold the Alt key while you press the Tab key until Netscape appears, then release both keys.

3. Position your pointer over any one of the pkz204g.exe links.

The URL in the status message area begins with "ftp://," indicating an FTP site, and ends with "/pkz204g.exe," the filename. The server and folder names in between will vary, depending upon which site you selected.

4. Click the **pkz204g.exe** link to open the Save As dialog box.

TROUBLE? If the Save As dialog box does not open and the transfer begins showing strange characters across the screen, your Netscape Helper list might be set incorrectly. Click the Stop button 🛑 on the toolbar to abort the link, then click Options, click General Preferences, click the Helpers tab, scroll down until you see the exe,bin line in the extensions column and click it, click the Save to Disk radio button, click the OK button, then repeat Step 4.

TROUBLE? If the Unknown File Type dialog box opens, click the Save to Disk button to open the Save As dialog box. Continue with Step 5.

TROUBLE? If you see an error message stating "FTP Error Could not login to FTP server." the site you linked to is busy. Click the Back button ⬅ on the toolbar to return to the Archie Search Results page and try a different site. If no other sites are listed, click ⬅ until you return to the Global Marketers, Inc. page, and then repeat the query with a different Archie server.

5. Type **a:\pkzip\pkz204g.exe** in the File name text box to save the file you are transferring in the pkzip folder on your disk with the filename pkz204g.exe. See Figure 3-25.

Figure 3-25 ◀
Save As dialog
box

type filename here ————

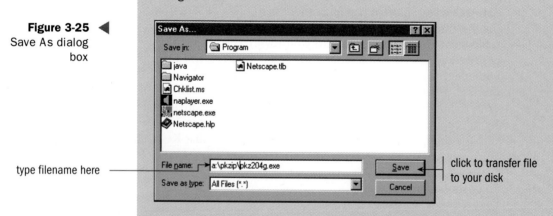

click to transfer file
to your disk

6. Make sure your Student Disk is in drive A or the appropriate disk drive, then press the **Enter** key. The pkzip file downloads to your disk.

With the pkzip file saved to your disk, you're almost ready to uncompress it. But first, you want to make sure it doesn't have a virus.

Detecting Viruses

Files stored in public directories are highly subject to viruses. Any file that you download from an anonymous FTP site should be checked. A **virus** is a destructive program code embedded, or hidden, in an executable file. When you run an infected program, the virus can affect the performance of your computer, display messages or images on your screen, or even erase your hard disk.

In order to protect your computer, you should run an anti-virus program on every file you download and every disk you get from someone else. An **anti-virus program** looks for suspicious series of commands or codes within an executable file and compares them to a list of known virus codes. If the program finds a match, it removes the virus from your disk. If you haven't opened an infected file, then it doesn't infect your computer. Anti-virus programs are frequently updated because new viruses are constantly appearing. You can download current anti-virus programs from the Internet.

In order to protect its computers, Global Marketers requires that an anti-virus program check every downloaded file before uncompressing and using it.

To scan for a virus:

1. Click the **Start** button on the Windows 95 taskbar, then click **Run** to open the Run dialog box.

   TROUBLE? If you are using an earlier version of Windows whenever you see these directions, press and hold the Alt key while you press the Tab key until you see Program Manager, then release both keys. Click File, then click Run. In Step 2, use the Command line text box instead of the Open text box.

2. Type **c:\dos\mwav.exe** or the name of the anti-virus program on your computer in the Open text box, then click the **OK** button to launch the anti-virus program. See Figure 3-26.

Figure 3-26 ◀
Completed Run
dialog box

type filename here ⎯⎯⎯⎯

click to start program ⎯⎯⎯⎯

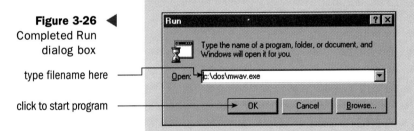

   TROUBLE? If you receive an error message stating the file cannot be found, the program name might be entered incorrectly; repeat Step 2. If you get the same error message, then mwav.exe might not be installed on your computer. Ask your instructor or technical support person if there is a different anti-virus program installed on your computer. If so, repeat Steps 1 and 2 using that program name instead of mwav.exe (your procedure will vary from Steps 3 through 5); if not, skip to the "Self-Extracting a File" section.

3. Click **drive A** or the appropriate drive, then click the **Detect and Clean** button to start the anti-virus program. When all the files on your Student Disk are scanned, a Statistics dialog box opens, showing the results of the scan. The Infected column indicates that no viruses were detected in the downloaded uncompression program. See Figure 3-27.

Figure 3-27 ◀
Virus scan
statistics

disk was scanned

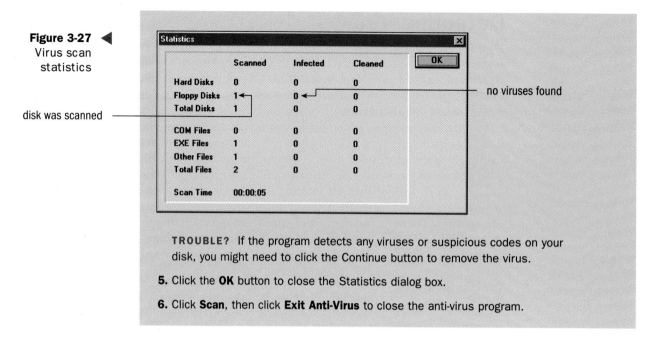

no viruses found

TROUBLE? If the program detects any viruses or suspicious codes on your disk, you might need to click the Continue button to remove the virus.

5. Click the **OK** button to close the Statistics dialog box.

6. Click **Scan**, then click **Exit Anti-Virus** to close the anti-virus program.

The pkz204g file isn't infected with any virus, so you can run it on the computers at Global Marketers.

Self-Extracting a File

Global Marketers doesn't have a program to uncompress downloaded programs, which is why you downloaded pkz204g.exe for the office to use. Although pkz204g contains a series of compressed files, Global Marketers won't need a separate program to uncompress it, because it is a self-extracting file. A **self-extracting file** uncompresses or restores its compressed files without a separate uncompression utility.

You'll restore the pkz204g file so that Global Marketers can use it.

To self-extract a file:

1. Click the **Start** button on the Windows 95 taskbar, then click **Run** to open the Run dialog box.

2. Type **a:\pkzip\pkz204g.exe** in the Open text box.

3. Click the **OK** button to begin the self-extraction. A DOS window opens, because the program is a DOS utility, and shows the steps for uncompressing the file. See Figure 3-28.

Figure 3-28
DOS window
with
uncompressed
files

list of files in
compressed
pkz204g.exe

message appears
when files are
uncompressed

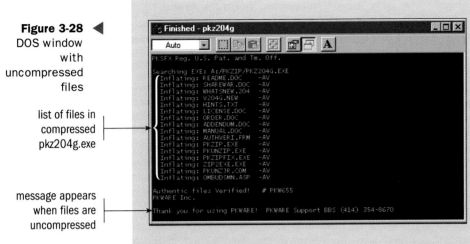

TROUBLE? If you receive an error message stating the file could not be found, the program name might not be typed correctly. Repeat Step 2.

TROUBLE? If you receive an error message stating the disk is full, both the compressed file and the extracted files do not fit onto your disk. Return to the section "Downloading an Uncompression Program" and repeat all the steps to this point using a *blank*, formatted high-density disk.

4. Click the **Close** button ⊠ to exit the window.

TROUBLE? If you are using an earlier version of Windows, the DOS window closes automatically. Continue with Step 5.

You should verify that the files opened into the pkzip folder on your disk.

5. Click the right mouse button on the Start button in the Window 95 taskbar, then click **Explore**. Scroll up the All Folders pane, click **3½ Floppy (A:)**, then double-click the **pkzip** folder. Your list of extracted files should match the list shown in Figure 3-29.

Figure 3-29
List of
extracted files

file Global
Marketers wants

text instructions that
accompany most
downloaded programs

licensing or ordering
information

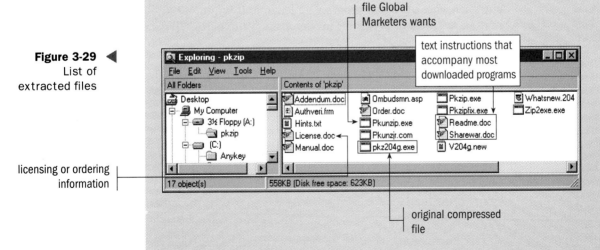

original compressed
file

TROUBLE? If you are using an earlier version of Windows, locate and double-click the File Manager icon, click the A: button, and double-click the Pkzip folder. Your list of extracted files should match the list shown in Figure 3-29.

6. Click the **Close** button ⊠ in the upper-right corner of the Explorer window to close the window.

TROUBLE? If your window does not have a Close button, click File, then click Exit.

Now that you have an uncompression program, you'll be able to uncompress any other files you download for Global Marketers. The uncompression program, like most programs you can download from the Internet, is not a free program, but you can use it for a short period of time to see how it works. If you decide to keep it, you'll have to purchase it.

Using Shareware

A program that you can try before buying is called **shareware**. The people who write these programs enjoy sharing their ideas and creations, hence the name *share*ware. The authors of shareware are not employees of software companies, but, rather, college students, professionals, or hobbyists, who had an idea for a program or an interest in programming. The Internet provides a convenient and inexpensive way to market a program and get feedback on its features.

The authors make their programs available for a free trial; if you decide to keep the program, you must send the author a fee, as outlined in the text file attached to the program. To help ensure that people send in the appropriate fee after a trial period, many authors usually distribute a demonstration version, which might have disabled features. When you register and purchase the program, you'll receive a full working version and information about **updates**, or revisions, to the program. Registering and sending payment for any shareware you plan to keep and use will encourage shareware authors to continue to write new versions or create other programs.

Kevin asks you to find some other program that will help Global Marketers to grow and offer quality service to its clients—for example, project-management programs or programs relating to graphics might be helpful for a company involved with advertising. Before he purchases any program, Kevin wants to be able to evaluate it and determine if it's appropriate for the company—like you are doing with the pkzip program. He suggests that you look for shareware programs.

Browsing for Shareware

Sometimes you will know the filename of the program you want to download, but more often you will only know what type of program you want. Archie servers are helpful only when you know the program's filename. If you don't know the filename, you can browse categories of programs in Web pages of hypertext links to a variety of FTP sites and programs.

Because the goal of Global Marketers is to prepare online, international advertising, several kinds of programs might be useful. You'll look at different types of shareware available on the Internet while browsing through some Web pages dedicated to cataloging FTP files by topic.

To browse for shareware:

1. If necessary, click the **Netscape** button on the Windows 95 taskbar to switch to the Global Marketers, Inc. page.

    TROUBLE? If you are using an earlier version of Windows, press and hold the Alt key while you press the Tab key until you see Netscape, then release both keys.

    TROUBLE? If Netscape is no longer an open program, then relaunch Netscape.

    TROUBLE? If you don't see the Global Marketers, Inc. page, click the Location box, type http://www.vmedia.com/cti/NewPerspectives/tiun in the Location text box, then press the Enter key. Click the Tutorial 3 link, then click Global Marketers, Inc.

2. Scroll down until you see the "Shareware Browsers" section.

3. Click the **Jumbo!** link to connect to a list of programs. See Figure 3-30.

Figure 3-30 ◀
Jumbo
shareware page

click category for
more detailed listings

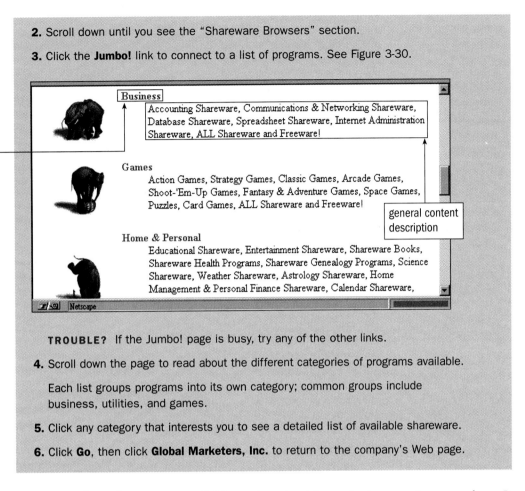

TROUBLE? If the Jumbo! page is busy, try any of the other links.

4. Scroll down the page to read about the different categories of programs available.

Each list groups programs into its own category; common groups include business, utilities, and games.

5. Click any category that interests you to see a detailed list of available shareware.

6. Click **Go**, then click **Global Marketers, Inc.** to return to the company's Web page.

The number of programs available to download from the Internet is tremendous. It would take weeks to research every program link. For now, you'll download one program to examine it.

The process is the same for each shareware program you want to evaluate:

- Download a copy of the program and scan the file for viruses.

- Uncompress, or unzip, the file.

- Install the program if necessary.

- Test the program.

- Send payment if you decide to keep the program past the trial period.

Downloading Shareware

Global Marketers plans to use graphics (photographs, line art, clipart, and so on) in its online advertising as well as in printed materials. Graphics on the Internet commonly are in the .gif format, which you can copy and save. However, because many word-processing programs cannot interpret .gif files, you can't insert them into a document. Instead, many programs recognize the .bmp, or bitmap, format, which you can modify with a common Windows painting program, such as Paint or Paintbrush. As a result, there are programs to convert .gif files to .bmp files, which make the images more versatile.

You think a program that converts one file to another will help make Global Marketers more productive and competitive. You decide to download this program to evaluate it.

To download shareware:

1. Create a folder named **gif** on your Student Disk to keep this program separate from the uncompression program.

2. Scroll down the Global Marketers, Inc. page until you see the "Shareware Trial" heading.

3. Click any of the **gif2bmp.zip** Graphics Conversion Shareware links to begin downloading the file. The Save As dialog box opens.

   TROUBLE? If the Unknown File Type dialog box opens, your installation of Netscape is not configured for downloading zipped files. Click the Save File button to open the Save As dialog box.

   TROUBLE? If you receive an error message stating "FTP Error Could not login to FTP server." then the site is busy. Click the Back button 🔲 on the toolbar and click a different link.

4. Click the **Save as type** list arrow, then click **All files (*.*)** to select the file format.

5. Type **a:\gif\gif2bmp.zip** in the File name text box to name the file being saved to your disk.

6. Press the **Enter** key. The file transfers to your disk, and the Save As dialog box closes.

Now that you've downloaded the graphics-conversion program, you want to make sure it doesn't carry a virus. You'll scan for viruses now.

To scan for a virus:

1. Click the **Start** button on the Windows 95 taskbar, then click **Run** to open the Run dialog box.

2. Type **c:\dos\mwav.exe** or the name of the anti-virus program on your computer in the Open text box, then click the **OK** button to launch the anti-virus program.

   TROUBLE? If you receive an error message stating the file cannot be found, the program name might be entered incorrectly. Repeat Step 2. If you get the same error message, ask your instructor or technical support person if a different anti-virus program is installed on your computer. If so, repeat Step 2 using that program's name. If not, skip to the "Unzipping a File" section.

3. Click **drive A** or the appropriate disk drive, then click the **Detect and Clean** button to start the anti-virus program.

4. When the scan is complete, click the **OK** button.

5. Click **Scan**, then click **Exit** to close the anti-virus program.

The file is clean; it does not contain a virus, so you can uncompress the file.

Unzipping a File

Most shareware that you download must be **unzipped**, or uncompressed, with an unzip utility into an .exe file that you can run. Any file with a .zip extension needs to be unzipped before you can use it. Earlier, you downloaded pkunzip.exe, an uncompression utility that came with pkz204g.zip, which you can use to unzip the graphics-conversion program.

To unzip a file:

1. Click the **Start** button on the Windows 95 taskbar, then click **Run** to open the Run dialog box.

2. Type **a:\pkzip\pkunzip.exe a:\gif\gif2bmp.zip a:\gif** in the Open text box to indicate that you want the pkunzip program in the pkzip folder to expand the compressed graphics-conversion program in the gif folder on your Student Disk. See Figure 3-31.

Figure 3-31 ◀
Unzipping a file

uncompression utility
to run

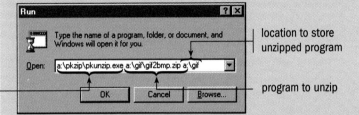

location to store
unzipped program

program to unzip

3. Click the **OK** button to unzip the file. Because the program is a DOS utility, a DOS window opens and shows the steps being completed to unzip the file.

   TROUBLE? If you receive an error message stating the file could not be found, the program name might not be typed correctly. Repeat Step 2. If you get the same message, repeat all the steps from the section "Downloading Shareware".

   TROUBLE? If you receive an error message stating the disk is full, you cannot fit the extracted files onto your current Student Disk. Because you already uncompressed the pkzip file, delete pkz204g.exe (the compressed file) from your disk to make room. If you need help, ask your instructor or technical support person.

4. When the file is unzipped, click the **Close** button ☒ to exit the DOS window if necessary.

The file is unzipped and ready to run.

Testing Shareware

Now that you've unzipped the graphics-conversion program, you can try it out. You'll use the software to convert a sample .gif image that is part of the Global Marketers, Inc. page to a .bmp file.

To convert a file using the graphics-conversion program:

1. If necessary, return to the Global Marketers, Inc. page.

2. Click the right mouse button on the globe next to Test Image to open a shortcut menu. See Figure 3-32.

Figure 3-32 ◀
Shortcut menu

click to open Save As
dialog box

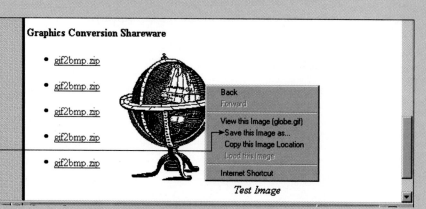

3. Click **Save this Image as** in the shortcut menu to open the Save As dialog box.

4. Type **a:\gif\sample.gif** in the File name text box to name the file, then click the **Save** button. The image file is saved to your disk in the same folder as the graphics-conversion program.

5. Click the **Start** button on the Windows 95 taskbar, then click **Run** to open the Run dialog box.

6. Type **a:\gif\gif2bmp.exe sample.gif** in the Open text box, and then click the **OK** button to run the graphics-conversion program on the Test Image file. A DOS window opens and shows the steps that occur.

   TROUBLE? If you receive an error message stating the file could not be found, the program name might be typed incorrectly. Repeat Step 6. If the message appears again, check the list of files in the gif folder on your disk. If you are missing the file gif2bmp.doc or gif2bmp.exe, repeat the steps in the section "Unzipping a File." If you are missing the file sample.gif, repeat Steps 1 through 6.

7. When the graphic is converted, close the DOS window, if necessary.

The image file is converted, but you cannot determine if the new file will open in programs commonly used at Global Marketers. As a check, you decide to open the image in the simple Paint program that comes with Windows.

To verify the conversion:

1. Click the **Start** button on the Windows 95 taskbar, position the pointer over **Programs** to open the Programs menu, then position the pointer over **Accessories** to open that menu.

2. Click **Paint** to start the program.

   TROUBLE? If you are using an earlier version of Windows, double-click the Paintbrush icon. If you cannot find either the Paint or the Paintbrush program, ask you instructor or technical support person for help.

3. Click **File**, then click **Open** to display the Open dialog box.

4. Type **a:\gif\sample.bmp** in the File name text box. See Figure 3-33.

Figure 3-33 ◀
Open dialog box

type filename of converted image here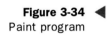

5. Press the **Enter** key, and the graphics file appears. See Figure 3-34.

bitmap (.bmp) version of the globe image

Figure 3-34 ◀
Paint program

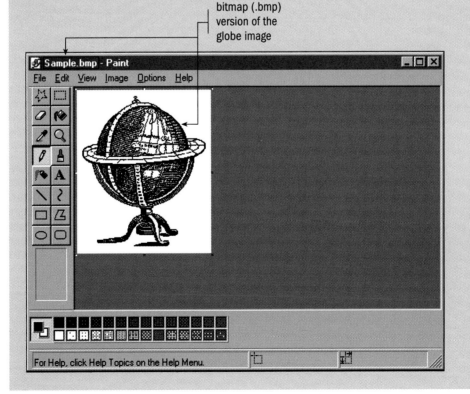

TROUBLE? If you receive an error message stating the file could not be found, you might have typed the filename incorrectly. Repeat Step 4. If you get the same message again, check the list of files on your disk. If sample.bmp is missing, repeat both sets of steps in this section.

The file opens without a problem in the Paint program. This program might be very useful for Global Marketers. You decide to show Kevin the program. Because you'll be leaving your computer for awhile, you exit both the Paint program and Netscape.

6. Click **File**, then click **Exit** to close the Paint program.

7. Click **File**, then click **Exit** to close Netscape.

Kevin is pleased with the graphics-conversion program and wants to test it with other programs the company uses, so you'll keep the shareware for its 30-day trial period. If the program continues to work well, the company will send payment to the shareware author as outlined in the accompanying text file. Kevin thanks you for your work so far. Both the graphics-conversion program and the unzip utility will be used frequently at Global Marketers. Kevin mentions that he's looking forward to seeing what shareware you will find next.

Quick Check

1. What does FTP mean?

2. The process of logging onto a remote computer and copying a file to your local computer is called _____.

3. When anyone can access the files on a public directory, it is called a(n) _____ FTP site.

4. What are two benefits of compressing a file?

5. When you know the name of the program you want to find, the fastest way to locate a copy is by using a(n) _____ server.

6. True or False: Every file that has a .zip extension is self-extracting.

7. _____ is a program that can be copied and tested for free. You pay for it only if you decide to keep it.

8. True or False: To unzip a file, you click its hypertext link.

Tutorial Assignments

The employees at the three branch offices of Global Marketers, Inc. frequently telephone each other as well as their clients, who are located around the world. To minimize the number of times an international call is placed from Global Marketers (saving both time and money), employees must calculate the correct local time for the client they are trying to reach. This helps ensure that the employees call during the client's business hours when he or she is more likely to be available. To make things easier for the company's employees, Kevin Maki wants to download a shareware program that can display the local time for any city in the world. Kevin asks you to download a copy of tzv111.zip, run a virus scan, uncompress the program and test it. After you verify that it will do what he wants, Kevin will e-mail a copy of the compressed file to Jane and Megan at the European branch offices.

Do the following:

1. Create a new folder on your Student Disk called "time"; you should now have three folders on your Student Disk: pkzip, gif, and time.
2. If necessary, launch Netscape so you can download the timezone program.
3. Open the Web page at the URL http://www.vmedia.com/cti/NewPerspectives/tiun and then click the Tutorial Assignments and Case Problems link.
4. Scroll down until you see the Tutorial 3 Tutorial Assignments section for Global Marketers, Inc.
5. Click the Timezone shareware link to download the file tzv111.zip and then save it as "a:\time\tzv111.zip" on your Student Disk.
   Before you uncompress the program, you'll run a virus scan on your Student Disk.
6. Open the Run dialog box, type "c:\dos\mwav.exe" (or the name of your computer's anti-virus program) in the Open text box, then press the Enter key.
7. Click drive A or the appropriate disk drive on your computer, then click the Detect and Clean button.
8. When the scan on your Student Disk is complete, exit the anti-virus program. With the disk clean of any virus, you can unzip tzv111.zip using the pkunzip program on your Student Disk.
9. Open the Run dialog box again, type "a:\pkzip\pkunzip.exe a:\time\tzv111.zip a:\time", then press the Enter key.
10. If necessary, close the DOS window when the uncompression is finished.
    The timezone program is uncompressed on your Student Disk, so you can try it.
11. Open the Run dialog box again, type "a:\time\timezone.exe" in the Open text box, then press the Enter key.

12. Click the upper list arrow, then click a city in your time zone. The current date and time for your time zone appear to the right of your selection.
13. Click the lower list arrow, then click a country or city anywhere in the world outside your time zone. The current time in that country or city appears to the right of your selection.

Now that you've tried the timezone program, you'll send an e-mail with the timezone documentation file (readme.txt) attached.

14. Return to Netscape, click Window, then click Netscape Mail (the Timezone window remains visible).

15. Click the To Mail button, type your instructor's e-mail address in the Mail To text box, type "Timezone test" in the Subject text box, then type a brief message stating the country or city you selected and its current time. (If necessary, move the Timezone window out of the way.)

16. Click the Attach button, click the Attach File button, type "a:\time\readme.txt" in the File name text box, then press the Enter key.

17. Click the OK button, then click the Send button.

18. Close the Netscape Mail window, then exit Netscape.

19. Exit the Timezone program by clicking the clock, then clicking Close.

Case Problems

1. Locating an Anti-Virus Program for Bennett Accounting Terrance Bennett owns a small accounting firm and manages the computer network at his accounting firm. Many of his clients use Windows 95 so Terrance is switching some of his company's computers to Windows 95. He wants to install a Windows 95 anti-virus program on these computers before allowing other employees to download files. He wants to purchase the virus scanner created by the McAfee company, but doesn't know the name of the file or where to find it. Terrance also wants to update the anti-virus program installed on the computers running an earlier versions of Windows. This is important to help ensure that the program can detect and clean new viruses that have emerged since he last updated the anti-virus program.

After he locates and installs the new anti-virus programs, he needs to find information he can use to train Bennett employees about computer viruses and tell them what steps to take to protect their files. Terrance asks you to locate the McAfee Windows 95 anti-virus program and a more current anti-virus program for earlier versions of Windows, and obtain computer virus information he can use for training.

If necessary, launch Netscape, and then do the following:

1. Open the Web page at the URL http://www.vmedia.com/cti/NewPerspectives/tiun and then click the Tutorial Assignments and Case Problems link.

2. Scroll down until you see the Tutorial 3 Case Problems section for Bennett Accounting.

3. Use the links provided in this section to learn about viruses and tips to avoid them.

4. When you find a Web page you think contains information Terrance can use for training, save it to your Student Disk as a text file called "a:\virus.txt."

5. Find a Web site that has the McAfee Windows 95 anti-virus program. Add a bookmark to this Web page on the Bookmark file on your Student Disk. What is the name of the anti-virus program file?

6. Find a popular anti-virus program for earlier versions of Windows. Add a bookmark to this Web page on the Bookmark file on your Student Disk. At what Web site can you find this program?

7. Open the Mail window and prepare an e-mail message to send to your instructor; attach the a:\virus.txt file you saved to the e-mail.

8. Write a short message to your instructor; include the URLs of the two pages you bookmarked, one for Windows 95 and one for the earlier version of Windows, in the body of the message. *Hint:* In the Netscape window, copy the URL from the first Web page to the clipboard, then switch to the Mail Composition window and paste it into the message content area. Repeat this for the second Web page.

9. Send the e-mail message to your instructor, close the Mail window, and then exit Netscape.

10. If you are working on your own computer, create a folder called "c:\virus" on your computer's hard disk, then download and uncompress the appropriate anti-virus program for your computer into the folder you just created.

2. Finding Compression Programs for Keller's Graphic Arts Candace Sullivan is a graphics artist employed at Keller's Graphic Arts. She frequently copies graphics files that she's created to a disk in order to show colleagues and clients her work. Because graphics files are typically large, Candace wants to compress groups of graphics files into one compressed file before copying them to minimize the number of disks she'll need. Although the pkzip program can compress groups of files, Candace prefers a Windows utility because it is easier to use. Candace read in a recent graphics magazine that the shareware program WinZip 6.0 is a good Windows compression utility. It comes in two versions: winzip95.exe for Windows 95 and wz60wn16.exe for earlier versions of Windows. Candace has two computers, one with Windows 3.1 and the other with Windows 95, so she asks you to find where she can obtain copies of both programs. Candace wants you to find and save the price and ordering information for both WinZip 6.0 programs so she can pay the shareware registration fee after evaluating them.

If necessary, start Netscape, and then do the following:

1. Open the Web page at the URL http://www.vmedia.com/cti/NewPerspectives/tiun and then click the Tutorial Assignments and Case Problems link.

2. Scroll down until you see the Tutorial 3 Case Problems section for Keller's Graphic Arts.

3. Click any Archie server and type "winzip95.exe" in the query text box. Submit (or start) the search; from the results list write down the name of an FTP host where you can find the file.

4. Click any Archie server and type "wz60wn16.exe" in the query text box. Submit the search; from the results list, write down the name of an FTP host where you can find the file.

5. Open the WinZip page at the URL http://www.winzip.com/. *Hint*: If the URL is not active, click Netscape's Net Search directory button and search for "winzip."

6. Use the Find command, to locate ordering information and then connect to that Web page.

7. What is the price for purchasing two copies of the WinZip program?

8. Save this Web page with the ordering information to your Student Disk as a text file called "a:\winzip.txt."

9. Open the Mail window, then click the To Mail button.

10. Prepare an e-mail message to send to your instructor. In the body of the message include the FTP host name where you located each version of WinZip and the price for purchasing two copies of WinZip. Attach a copy of the "a:\winzip.txt" file to the e-mail.

11. Send the e-mail message, close the Mail window, and then exit Netscape.

3. Retrieving an MPEG Viewer for CourseWare Online Bonnie Olson, an associate at CourseWare Online, develops computer-based training (CBT) programs that hospitals use to supplement the training of their medical technicians. The medical technicians that use CBT programs proceed through the material at their own pace. They select appropriate lessons, read the information on the computer monitor, and check their understanding by answering quiz questions Bonnie already incorporates sound and graphics in the material and wants to add video clips. Most Internet video clips are stored in a compressed format called MPEG (Moving Pictures Expert Group), which must be viewed using an MPEG viewer program. Several MPEG viewers are available on the Internet, but Bonnie wants to try one called vmpeg because its copyright permits her to distribute it with her CBT programs. Bonnie asks you to download the vmpeg file, check it for viruses, uncompress the program, and test it.

If necessary, start Netscape, and then do the following:

1. Copy your Student Disk for Session 3.2 onto a blank, formatted disk. Delete the gif folder to make room for the MPEG viewer files. Create a folder on the disk called vmpeg. *Hint:* To copy an entire disk to another disk use the File menu in My Computer for Windows 95, or the Disk menu in File Manager for earlier versions of Windows.

2. Open the Web page at the URL http://www.vmedia.com/cti/NewPerspectives/tiun and then click the Tutorial Assignments and Case Problems link.

3. Scroll down until you see the Tutorial 3 Case Problems section for CourseWare Online.

4. Download the vmpeg.zip program into the vmpeg folder on your disk.

5. Run a virus scan on your disk. *Hint:* Open the Run dialog box, and then type "c:\dos\mwav.exe" or the name of the anti-virus program on your computer into the Open text box. When the scan is finished, exit the anti-virus program.

6. Unzip vmpeg.zip using the pkunzip program on your disk. *Hint:* Open the Run dialog box, type "a:\pkzip\pkunzip.exe a:\vmpeg\vmpeg.zip a:\vmpeg" in the Open text box and press the Enter key. If pkunzip and vmpeg.zip are not in these folders or drive A, use their correct locations. If necessary, close the DOS window.

7. Run the vmpeg viewer from the Run dialog box. *Hint:* In the Open text box type "a:\vmpeg\vmpegnwg.exe" and then press the Enter key.

8. Open and play the demo video file called "a:\vmpeg\demo.mpg" using the viewer's menu options.

9. Exit the vmpeg viewer program.

10. Switch to Netscape and open the Mail window. Prepare an e-mail message to send to your instructor; mention that you successfully uncompressed the zipped file and attach the vmpeg documentation file called "a:\vmpeg\vmpeg.doc."

11. Send the e-mail message, close the Mail window, and then exit Netscape.

4. Scavenger Hunts on the World Wide Web The WWW contains programs that cover a wide range of needs, including financial programs, graphics programs, and compression programs. Use any Archie server and shareware browser available on the Global Marketers, Inc. page to find the following files on the WWW. As you locate each file, write its location into a text file that you create in a word-processing program such as Windows NotePad or Windows 95 WordPad.

1. Create a text file named "a:\case4.txt" on your Student Disk using a word-processing program such as Windows NotePad or Windows 95 WordPad. Leave this program open and switch between it and Netscape as necessary.

2. Use a shareware browser to obtain a list of Windows 95 screen saver utilities. Switch to the text file, add this list, save the text file, then return to Netscape.

3. A useful program for viewing JPEG graphics files is Lview31.exe. The program is archived in a file called Lview31.zip. Where can you find this file on the Web? Switch to the text file, add the location, save the text file, then return to Netscape.

4. Several programs provide a Windows GIF viewer. One of the more popular is Wingif. What is the exact filename for Wingif? Switch to the text file, add the filename, save the text file, then return to Netscape. *Hint*: If you don't know the exact filename of a program, use an Archie server that allows you to select "regular expression" as the type of search, rather than an exact match.

5. You can access anonymous FTP sites directly with an FTP program. This type of program allows you to upload, as well as download, files to an FTP site. One such program is archived in a file called ws_ftp.zip. Find this file on the Web. Switch to the text file, add this location, and save the text file.

6. Close the word-processing program and return to Netscape.

7. Prepare an e-mail message to send to your instructor; attach the a:\case4.txt file converted to plain text.

8. Send the e-mail message, close the Mail window, and then exit Netscape.

Lab Assignment

This Lab Assignment is designed to accompany the interactive Course Lab called E-mail. **To start the Lab using Windows 95,** click the Start button on the Windows 95 taskbar, point to Programs, point to Course Labs, point to New Perspectives Applications, and click E-Mail. **To start the Lab using Windows 3.1,** double-click the Course Labs for the Internet group icon to open a window containing the Lab icons, then double-click the E-mail icon. If you do not see Course Labs on your Windows 95 Programs menu, or if you do not see the Course Labs for the Internet group icon in your Windows 3.1 Program Manager window, see your instructor or technical support person.

E-Mail E-mail that originates on a local area network with a mail gateway can travel all over the world. That's why it is so important to learn how to use it. In this Lab you use an e-mail simulator, so even if your school computers don't provide you with e-mail service, you will know the basics of reading, sending, and replying to electronic mail.

1. Click the Steps button to learn how to work with E-mail. As you proceed through the Steps, answer all of the Quick Check questions that appear. After you complete the Steps, you will see a Quick Check summary report. Follow the instructions on the screen to print this report.

2. Click the Explore button. Write a message to re@films.org. The subject of the message is "Picks and Pans." In the body of your message, describe a movie you have recently seen. Include the name of the movie, briefly summarize the plot, and give it a thumbs up or a thumbs down. Print the message before you send it.

3. Look in your In Basket for a message from jb@music.org. Read the message, then compose a reply indicating that you will attend. Carbon copy mciccone@music.org. Print your reply, including the text of JB's original message before you send it.

4. Look in your In Basket for a message from leo@sports.org. Reply to the message by adding your rating to the text of the original message as follows:

Equipment:	Your Rating:
Rollerblades	2
Skis	3
Bicycle	1
Scuba gear	4
Snow mobile	5

   Print your reply before you send it.

5. Go into the lab with a partner. You should each log into the E-mail Lab on different computers. Look at the Addresses list to find the user ID for your partner. You should each send a short E-mail message to your partner. Then, you should check you mail message from your partner. Read the message and compose a reply. Print your reply before you send it. *Note: Unlike a full-featured mail system, the e-mail simulator does not save mail in mailboxes after you log off.*

Answers to Quick Check Questions

Session 1.1

1 False

2 The Web page you see when Netscape starts or the first document that opens when you connect to another site.

3 False

4 URL

5 link

6 status bar; status indicator

7 Document: Done

8 abort

Session 1.2

1 True

2 http, ftp, gopher

3 No. Domain names are case sensitive.

4 The URL might be typed incorrectly. The Web page might have been deleted or renamed.

5 Forward, Back, Home

6 speed, quality

7 False

8 attachment

9 Online help

Session 2.1

1 surfing

2 False

3 What's Cool

4 increased

5 theme or subject

6 history log

7 bookmark

8 False

Session 2.2

1 search engine

2 or; any document with either word of the query would be included

3 False

4 Gopher

5 Spiders

6 navigational

7 text or .txt

8 True

Session 3.1

1 user ID; host name

2 Address Book

3 False

4 Cc

5 password

6 they are returned undelivered

7 False

8 False

Session 3.2

1 File Transfer Protocol

2 downloading

3 anonymous

4 smaller size of file; decreased time to transfer file

5 Archie

6 False

7 Shareware

8 False

Index

Netscape Navigator **Task Reference**

Address Book, use	NS 92	From Message Composition window, click ▣, click desired entry, click To	
Address Book file, import	NS 92	From Address Book window, click File, Import	
Address Book file, save	NS 91	From Address Book window, click File, Save As	
Address Book list, add item	NS 90	From Address Book window, drag item to desired list	
Address Book list, create	NS 90	From Address Book window, click Item, Add List	
Address Book window, open	NS 88	Click Window, Address book	
Attachment, include inline	NS 94	From Message Composition window, click View, Attachments as Links to toggled off if necessary	attached files included in body of message
Attachment, save	NS 98	From Message Composition window, click Attachment at end of message body	saves attachment independently of message
Bookmark, access	NS 55	Click Bookmarks, click desired Web page title	
Bookmark, add	NS 54	Click Bookmarks, Add Bookmark	saves bookmark for current page
Bookmark file, create	NS 53	Click Bookmarks, Go to Bookmarks, File, Save As	stores bookmarks in independent file
Bookmark file, open	NS 53	Click Bookmarks, Go to Bookmarks, File, Open	to use an alternate Bookmark file
Clipboard, copy to	NS 76	Select text, click Edit, Copy	
Directory Buttons, show	NS 18	Click Options, Show Directory Buttons	
Document, mail	NS 35	Click File, Mail Document	
File, download	NS 107	Click hypertext link for file	for software and compressed files
File, open	NS 16	Click File, Open File	
File, uncompress with pkunzip program	NS 115	Click Start, Run, type a:\pkunzip\pkunzip.exe *filename*	*filename* is the name of compressed file
Helper, set		Click Options, General Preferences, Helper Apps	add helper programs to Helper list
History log, use	NS 51	Click Go, click page to return to	
Image, save	NS 116	Click right mouse button on image, click Save this Image as	saves image to new file

Netscape Navigator **Task Reference**

Images, auto load	NS 18	Click Options, Auto Load Images if necessary to toggle on	
Images, load on demand	NS 32	Click 🖾	Auto Load option must be toggled off
Location, open	NS 27	Click 🖾, type URL, press Enter	
Location box, show	NS 18	Click Options, Show Location to toggle on if necessary	
Mail, delete	NS 101	From Mailbox window, select mail, click 🖾	
Mail, empty trash	NS 101	From Mailbox window, click File, Empty Trash Folder	
Mail, forward	NS 99	From Mailbox window, select mail, click 🖾	
Mail, get	NS 95	From Mailbox window, click 🖾	
Mail, read	NS 96	From Mailbox window, click Inbox folder, click message's subject	
Mail, reply	NS 97	From Mailbox window, select mail, click 🖾	
Mail, save message	NS 100	From Message Composition window, select mail, click File, Save As	
Mail, send	NS 85	From Mailbox window, click 🖾	
Mail Preferences, set identity	NS 83	Click Options, Mail and News Preferences, Identity, type user ID and full name	
Mail Preferences, set servers	NS 83	Click Options, Mail and News Preferences, Servers, type SMTP and POP servers	
Mailbox window, open	NS 85	Click Window, Netscape Mail	
Netscape, exit	NS 24	Click File, Exit	
Page, print	NS 34	Click 🖾	
Page, print preview	NS 33	Click File, Print Preview	
POP server, set		See Mail Preferences, set servers	
Source, view	NS 19	Click View, Document Source	
STMP, set		See Mail Preferences, set servers	
Toolbar, show	NS 18	Click Options, Show Toolbar to toggle on	
User ID, set		See Mail Preferences, set identity	